ACCELERATE
YOUR DESTINY

ENJOY GREAT FAMILY RELATIONSHIPS,
FINANCIAL FREEDOM &
BUSINESS SUCCESS!

HENRY A. PENIX

insight *i* publishing group
Tulsa, Oklahoma

ACCELERATE YOUR DESTINY

Accelerate Your Destiny by Henry A. Penix
Published by Insight Publishing Group
8801 S. Yale, Suite 410
Tulsa, OK 74137
918-493-1718

Scripture quotations marked NKJV are from the New King James Version of the Bible Copyright ©1979, 1980, 1982 by Thomas Nelson Inc., publishers. Used by permission.

Scripture quotations marked KJV are from the King James Version of the Bible.

Scripture quotations marked NIV are from the New International Version of the Bible. Copyright © 1973, 1978, 1984 by International Bible Society. Used by permission of Zondervan Publishing House.

Cover design by Jeffrey Mobley

ISBN 1-930027-44-3
Library of Congress catalog card number: 2001095107

Printed in the United States of America

TABLE OF CONTENTS

<u>WORKBOOK</u>
5 KEYS TO ACCELERATE YOUR DESTINY

DEDICATION

I would like to dedicate this book first to my family:

Laurie, my lovely wife without whom none of this would have happened who kept the faith and worked so hard in keeping our family, business, and marriage together. Thank you and I love you more than you could imagine.

Zac, my first child, who kept me in line and always gave me great business advise.

Olivia, my second child, who is and will continue to be "my very best friend."

Madison, my third child who can light up any room with her joy and happiness—my life would not have been complete without you.

To my mother and father who always believed in me and supported everything (well almost everything) that I set out to do—my father who taught me how to relate to the public and run my own business, thanks dad—I love you.

To my mom who always tried to keep me out of trouble with my father and who led an exemplary life that I tried to follow. Your love and forgiveness in any situation was Godlike—I love you mom.

To my sister Ronda, who served as a great punching bag growing up until she started sharpening her fingernails—I have seen the almost insurmountable adversity you have overcome. Congratulations on becoming a great wife, mother (to my favorite niece Jewelia), sister, and friend.

To my "Nanny" and "Grandpa" who are no longer with us, but were very instrumental parts of my life.

To Laurie's mom, Carol, who always helped and supported our efforts.

To Laurie's dad, Townley, for allowing me to marry his daughter—thanks for your support with legal advice as well.

And last but certainly not least the one lady who helped back our first purchase and helped make possible all that followed, Ethel "Granny" Houchin (1901-1996)—a lady who would tell you like it is. Thanks for loving me and my family and treating me like one of your own.

ACKNOWLEDGMENTS

I would like to acknowledge the following people:

John Mason and the staff at Insight Publishing—for holding our hand and making our dream of writing this book a reality,

Brian Mast—for diligently completing this project in a timely fashion with keystrokes of inspiration and a heart of gold,

the staff, past and present, of Koala Care Preschool and Early Learning Centers and all the parents and students of Koala Care,

Michelle (Mimi)—a great regional director and her husband Brian "gets the job done" Hayes—a great fisherman who can hook the biggest,

Sandy Bjornson—the first banker who finally said "yes" and believed in us,

Brad Thompson—our banker who continued to carry the banking torch,

Linda Parish—our banker who helped with the transitions,

Phyllis—our first teacher and Bill Hardin—her husband who always helped with anything that needed to be done,

Keith Neal —owner of Keith Neal Construction, one of the finest builders around and his great crew—thanks for recommending the Owasso site to us, for making our dream home come true, and for teaching us to catch fish,

Kenneth and Charlotte Lawless—thank you for advising us in the beginning,

Alan McCormick—who spoiled me with private accounting services and taught me how to coach soccer. Thank you so much for your help during our transition,

Byron Davis—who helped maintain a peaceful environment with words and songs of encouragement,

Gary Crouch—my first CPA who gave me many lessons in accounting,

Stanfield, O'dell, and Greg Entwhistle—for helping carry the accounting torch,

Carlton and Gina Pearson—Pastor and First Lady of Higher Dimensions Family Church,

Billy Joe and Sharon Daugherty—Pastors of Victory Christian Center,

Leola Farmer—a great realtor,

Sharon—a great help in a time of need and her husband Richard Phillips,

Airco Heating and Air—for keeping us cool in the summer and warm in the winter,

John Penix—for building our fist addition,

Karen Loflin and Judy Kerr—for helping us get started,

all the crew at DHS in Tulsa, OK,

thanks to Jackie Cooper Imports in Tulsa—for all their help and support,

Mark and Robin Thompson—owners of Thompson Portrait Design Studio—for their help, support, and all the great pictures they took,

David Cameron—for his legal advice and expertise,

Dan Holmes and Jerry Reeves—for insuring that I sleep well at night,

Sam Arndt—for growing with us and helping us whenever possible,

and hundreds of others that we didn't mention who were an integral part in making our dreams come true—Thank you all!

Read what others are saying about Accelerate Your Destiny:

"Henry Penix's new book, *Accelerate Your Destiny* will not leave you the way it found you! It's proven principles will touch every area of your life with insight, ideas, and inspiration. No matter where you find yourself in life, this book will help take you to the next level."

John Mason, author of the national best-seller, *An Enemy Called Average*

"I will never forget the day Henry walked into my office. My original perception was that of an honest young man with a lot of dreams. He knew exactly what he wanted to do with his business. I am convinced that Henry's hard work and honesty are what made him a succuss. It was not luck. I am proud to be associated with him."

Sandy Bjornson
President—Community Bank and Trust

"Of all the success stories I've heard, I can only think of few that carry the impact that Henry Penix's does. Hearing about the journey that Henry and his wife made, to get where they are today, a place of success, really touched me personally. *Accelerate Your Destiny* reveals Henry's heart for God, his trust of Him in business, and his eloquence in communicating how God worked in and through his life. His life is a tremendous testimony!"

Peter Lowe
President and CEO of Peter Lowe International
Success Seminars

INTRODUCTION

Have you ever asked yourself: What am I doing with my life? Where am I headed? Why is life such a struggle? How will I ever pay all the bills? Why am I even here on earth? Why did I marry this person? How can I make enough money that I won't have to work? Why, when I seem to have enough money, am I not happy?

These are some of the questions I used to ask myself every day. Then slowly, over a period of time, I began to find answers through a process of personal revelations. Most of the revelations came from what I had been taught during my childhood as the "right thing to do" but had been pushed aside during my teenage years. My way was better, faster, and more exciting. I wanted to be happy and the "good life" would get me what I desired…or so I thought.

As a result, I've been to the bottom of the bottom many times. If you've been there too, then we can relate. You and I both know that we don't want to remain down there. Thankfully, we don't have to!

Today, different questions go through my head: How did I end up with such an incredible family? How is it that my once horrible marriage is now a great marriage? I'm retired and debt free at thirty-six years of age—why doesn't everyone live this type of life? How do you explain:

◈ Starting with a run-down failing business and turning it into a 20 million-dollar success?
◈ Having three wonderful children who are all currently testing in the top three percent of the nation?
◈ Owning my dream home built on twenty-five acres of prime real estate?
◈ Having all my broken family relationships healed and returned to a better-than-before status?
◈ Having health, peace, and joy in our family like never before?
◈ Lending to people instead of borrowing?

I've started to ask myself one additional question: how can I help other people live this incredible life? *That is the reason for this book.*

Included at the back of this special edition is a workbook that will help you apply what you will learn after reading this book to your own unique situation. *It is the same workbook I used that brought about the changes in my life!* To get what you've never gotten, you have to do what you've never done. Remember that the definition of insanity is doing the same thing over and over, yet expecting different results!

Make a change today. Take action, read this book, and complete the workbook. I promise you that your life will never be the same!

CHAPTER ONE

WE ALMOST DIDN'T MAKE IT!

Not everything in life comes as easy as you think it should. I thought life had dealt me a pretty good hand. I met the woman of my dreams, Laurie Lynn Price—*she's the best thing that ever happened to me*—but just after we met my life began to unravel.

Eight months later we were married, but our troubles had already begun. The next twelve months proved to be almost unbearable as we were tossed from one incredibly difficult and highly stressful situation to another. So much for a blissful first year of marriage! We kept saying, "Well, it can't get any worse than this!" and then it would.

To get a better perspective of our situation, consider the following stress test that I completed for my and Laurie's first year of marriage (keep in mind that the human body does not know the difference between a good stress and a bad stress).

LIFE'S STRESS TEST

Beside every stressful event that applied to us, I put an "x".

___Death of Spouse—*100 points*
_x_Change in work responsibilities—*29 points*
_x_Divorce—*73 points (my parents)*
___Trouble with in-laws—*29 points*
___Marital Separation—*65 points*
___Outstanding personal achievement—*28 points*

___Jail Term—*63 points*

_x_Spouse begins or stops work—*26 points*

_x_Death of close family member—*63 points*

_x_Starting or finishing school—*26 points*

_x_Personal injury or illness—*53 points*

_x_Change in living conditions—*25 points*

_x_Marriage—*50 points*

_x_Revision of personal habits—*24 points*

___Fired from work—*47 points*

___Trouble with boss—*23 points*

___Marital reconciliation—*45 points*

_x_Change in work hours, conditions—*20 points*

___Retirement—*45 points*

_x_Change in residence—*20 points*

___Change in family member's health—*44 points*

___Change in schools—*20 points*

_x_Pregnancy—*40 points*

_x_Change in recreational habits—*19 points*

___Sex difficulties—*39 points*

___Change in church activities—*19 points*

_x_Addition to family—*39 points*

_x_Change in social activities—*18 points*

_x_Business readjustment—*39 points*

_x_Mortgage or loan under $10,000—*17 points*

_x_Change in financial status—*38 points*

_x_Change in sleeping habits—*16 points*

___Death of close friend—*37 points*

_x_Change in number of family gatherings—*15 points*

_x_Change to a different line of work—*36 points*

___Change in eating habits—*15 points*

_x_Change in number of marital arguments—*35 points*

___Vacation—*13 points*

_x_Mortgage or loan over $10,000—*31 points*

_x_Christmas season—*12 points*
___Foreclosure of mortgage or loan—*30 points*
_x_Minor violations of the law—*11 points*

Copyright 1997 Conscious Living Foundation P.O. Box 9, Drain, OR 97435 (541) 836-2358 www.cliving.org

According to the scores at the end of the test, 0-149 points meant we had a low susceptibility to stress-related illness, 150-299 points meant we had a medium susceptibility, and 300 points and over meant we had a high susceptibility. ***Our grand total was a whopping 775!*** We gave the term "stressed-out" a whole new meaning!

Two months before we married we took out a loan to start a business that would primarily be Laurie's business. She went from not working one day to stressful, backbreaking twelve-hour workdays the next! When we got married we bought a little home for a great price, only to discover that there wasn't a single appliance in the entire house! I had to make myself look as good as I could on every credit application just to get a stove, refrigerator, washer, dryer, toaster, etc. It was not a pretty sight!

Our one income was minimized by the fact that her business took every extra dollar I made. We were suddenly responsible for making payroll, paying lease payments, and setting money aside for taxes, not to mention dealing with zoning requirements, local laws, forms to file, no working capital, and limited knowledge on how to run a business.

Within weeks of getting married, we had business debt, mortgage payments, car payments, insurance payments, and credit payments. To add insult to injury, I was forced to put our wedding rings (worth $130 combined!) on a twelve-month charge because I had no money!

Then the unexpected happened: Laurie discovered she was pregnant! She worked all the way through her pregnancy and continued almost immediately after little Zachry was born. Imagine being nine months pregnant working twelve-hour days!

All the while my parents were going through a separation that ultimately led to a divorce (Laurie's parents had divorced three years earlier). My dad also happened to be my pastor, which added more pressure to our already stressful life. Then on December 16, eleven months after we were married, what was left of our world fell apart. Laurie's eighteen-year-old brother, whom she had a large part in raising, was killed in a tragic and unnecessary car accident.

We were fighting, fighting for our very lives. We faced each issue head-on and kept working hard, believing that we would eventually come out the other end. We were responsible and pinched every penny we could, but sometimes even that wasn't enough.

How did we make it through? Honestly, it was nothing we did. All I could think was that maybe it was the result of people who said they had been praying for us? (How much they were praying we didn't find out until later.) Was God trying to tell me something through it all? Probably, but I had pretty much turned my back on God and the church a few years earlier and was not even trying to hear what He might be saying.

Amazingly enough, we were walking toward the plan and destiny for our lives—in spite of ourselves.

CHAPTER TWO

HUMBLE BEGINNINGS

On a whim, Laurie and I decided to go look at a run-down childcare center that was for sale. My mom had told us about it and we had discussed it over dinner before we went, but that was the extent of our pre-purchase planning. We arrived at night to inspect the building, which we later found was a bad mistake. The burned out light bulbs caught our attention, but one of the owners said, "Oh, we don't use the lights during the day, that is why we never noticed." We couldn't even see all the rooms, but we believed everything we were told.

The potential in the little childcare center excited us. Laurie, with all the bubbling creativity of a twenty-year-old, could "see" the classrooms filled with laughing children, brightly painted walls, clean carpets, computers, and more! And I, a twenty-two-year-old with very limited business experience (unless you count mowing lawns, working as a fitness instructor, managing the grounds of a condo, and working in a clothing store as qualifying experience) said, "Let's buy it!"

I had never taken out a loan before, but here I was asking for a business loan with zero working knowledge of a childcare center. And since I couldn't afford an attorney or other legal help, I handled all the paperwork, filings, and representing myself.

Laurie now says our first childcare center was "a dump," but back then we didn't have the foresight that we have now. We jumped headlong into the business, signed the papers, secured the loan, and purchased the run-down daycare center. We assumed responsibility for the building and the business on a Friday evening and the owners told us that they would be there on Monday to help with the transition. Unfortunately, they took the check and we never saw them again!

When the doors opened Monday morning at 6:30 a.m., we were on our own! Laurie quickly put nametags on the children to keep them straight and did her best to convince the parents that entrusting their children to a twenty-year-old whom they had never met was a good idea! It must have worked because all nine children came back the next day.

> **"PEOPLE FORGET THE LITTLE THINGS THAT YOU DO TO GET YOU WHERE YOU WANT TO GO."**
> –LAURIE PENIX

FALLING INTO OUR DESTINY

We probably would not have gotten into the business had my mom and dad not been in it (their small childcare center helped put my sister and I through college) and had Laurie not worked part-time in a childcare center when she was in high school. The decision to buy and operate a childcare center was both unexpected and naïve. Laurie had no plans to start a business, much less own one, and confesses, "I would have preferred a nice little dress shop."

However, she also loves a challenge. "From the moment I walked into the old building," she says, "I could see how it would look if we made change here, fixed that there, added this, etc. I could see it all, despite the cockroaches coming out of the cupboards and bathrooms that were so dirty I refused to use them."

We learned later that one of the keys to knowing you are walking in your destiny is the ability to "see" things where you are. Laurie, for example, could "see" the childcare center in its ideal format. This is more than just being a creative person. Some

16

people naturally imagine things in a completed state, and that is a powerful ability, but being able to "see" things goes even deeper. After working in the center for a little while, Laurie could "see" in her mind's eye exactly what the ideal floor plan of a childcare center would be like.

When we built an addition to our first little childcare center, we tried to match it with Laurie's floor plan. The result was spectacular! We ended up using a similar floor plan as the template from which all of our other centers were fashioned. We even had architects from national childcare centers trying to get into our building so that they could see it, measure it, and then copy it. Not bad for someone who didn't know much about construction, lighting, or ideal classroom sizes! When you're walking in your destiny, things that never seemed to work suddenly begin working.

Laurie also came up with a new name for the center: Koala Care. I thought it was a little silly, but she always liked Australia and thought the name had a warm feeling to it (she was right again!). We had a "Koala Care" magnetic business sign made that she proudly put on her old Mercedes station wagon (borrowed from her parents) that she would drive as she transported children from the childcare center to school and back.

Obviously, neither of us had training in what we did. We didn't even know we would be good at it. While we were trying to turn nothing into something, God was directing our steps. It was our destiny we were walking into, yet I knew personally that I was far from doing what I had been taught as a preacher's kid to do. God, in His own patient way, was using the childcare center and added responsibility to draw me back to a relationship with Him.

LEARN AS YOU GO

To be perfectly honest, we jumped into the business before we had done adequate research, preparation, and planning. When people ask for advice today, my first answer is this: "Don't start like we did!" However, I am quick to add that at least we made the decision to begin rather than analyzing the opportunity to death.

Someone wisely said that, "if you wait for perfect conditions, you will never get anything done." Some people refuse to jump into a business opportunity until they have first bought a brand new computer, new office space, a new phone line, a new desk, DSL service, etc., all before they have generated any money to pay for it! The truth is they don't want to have the business until they can get to the point where it is successful. (Nobody gives away profitable businesses these days!) And then there are those who sit and analyze the business opportunity until they are too scared to move.

I see both approaches like two planes sitting at the end of a runway. One plane is being washed, polished, cleaned, prepared, organized, outfitted, etc. while the other is about to barrel down the runway with only one engine, no fuel, no passengers, no landing gear, and no compass. Both are doomed to failure.

MOST BUSINESSES FAIL FOR LACK OF MONEY. BUT IF YOU WAIT UNTIL YOU CAN AFFORD EVERYTHING YOU WILL NEVER START.

Whatever the vision or dream we might have, we can't afford to sit until every last detail has been cross-examined and neither can we chase blindly after a good idea just because we are excited about it. Sadly, this aptly describes many people today, whether they are prospective business owners or not. Though there is a balance that every individual must find, *we certainly didn't find it before we started!*

However, we had several principles already in place (or quickly learned them!) that increased our chances of survival.

They were:

❖ **We took the first step.**

The most important factor is that we started. Yes, there were many more steps to take and decisions to make, but the first is always the most difficult.

❖ **We were willing to get dirty and work hard.**

We knew that without experience in running a childcare center, it would be just a matter of time before we failed at it. Success means jumping in, working hard, and getting dirty. That is what "sweat equity" is all about.

❖ **We were faithful with little.**

We understood that taking care of the little we had, no matter what it was or how insignificant it might be, was the surest way to prepare ourselves to handle even greater things.

❖ **We reinvested any income.**

Many small business owners use the money they make for their own legitimate personal needs. Instead, we turned it all back into the company for taxes, payroll, expansion, bonuses, bills, etc.

❖ **We were careful with our finances.**

When we were at our limit financially, we didn't go and buy a new car or go on a vacation. We knew our limits and operated within them. We went without things and skimped when we could (Laurie completely stopped buying clothes for a long time!).

◈ **We kept our word.**
We used to tell the parents that the centers would some day have computers, programs, and other benefits for the children. We then did whatever it took to fulfill our promises, even if at times we didn't "feel" like it.

◈ **We communicated.**
If something we planned didn't work out or ended up being impractical, we would go to everyone concerned and explain the situation and our decision. We wouldn't just ignore the fact.

◈ **We were patient.**
We were willing to take one small step at a time. We knew that taking each step would get us where we wanted to go—and that if we didn't take each step, we would never reach our goal.

There will always be an element of the unknown when people venture into something they are not 100 percent familiar or comfortable with. The sooner they accept this as a reality of life the better, but don't let that keep you from going for it!

People who try to figure everything out before they start need to realize that not even an airplane is perfectly on target when it takes off. In fact, throughout the entire flight the direction of the plane is constantly undergoing further corrections to compensate for wind speed, wind direction, weight, altitude, and fuel supply. If the plane simply

> "SHOW ME SOMEONE WHO HAS DONE SOMETHING WORTHWHILE, AND I'LL SHOW YOU SOMEONE WHO HAS OVERCOME ADVERSITY."
> – LOU HOLTZ

takes off and remains pointed toward its goal, even with the many corrections that must be made along the way, it will eventually land exactly where it originally planned to land.

That is the beauty of learning (and adjusting) as you go. The truth is, you will never really know if your plane will fly until *after* you take off! Once you've taken off, begin to adjust for obstacles that try to alter your course. Remain pointed toward your goal and you will eventually get there.

ACCELERATION = ONE SMALL STEP AT A TIME

Instead of focusing on what we did not have, we chose to focus on what we did have. Our approach was one small project at a time, one toy at a time, and one new student at a time. We walked methodically toward our goals. Little by little, what Laurie "saw" became a reality. Sometimes it took a little extra creativity to get where we wanted to go, but we eventually arrived.

Near the end of our first full year in the center, taxes were coming due and we didn't have enough money in the bank. Laurie was pregnant and her back hurt, but she came up with a great idea to stay open all night and have the children sleep over. So, on New Year's Eve, instead of going out and celebrating with our friends, we both worked all night to keep about thirty children entertained and safe. We even brought extra mattresses from our home for them to sleep on. At thirty-five dollars per child, we made over $1000, which was enough to pay our tax bill. Looking back, we simply did what it took and worked with what we had.

Another time, Laurie wanted to be a good employer and told her only employee to take the day off (it was the employee's birthday). This meant Laurie had to single-handedly keep everything going, including making lunch for everyone, and picking up students from school in the afternoon. She was exhausted by day's end, but she says, "It was important to me that she got the day off, so I did whatever it took to make it work out." We made it a point to always give back to those who were helping us.

During those long days (6:30 a.m. to 6 p.m.) of dealing with children who ranged in ages from six weeks to eleven years, while simultaneously trying to renovate a neglected childcare center into a profitable business, Laurie admits, "Some days I saw no light at the end of the tunnel."

ANY CONCEIVABLE PROBLEM CANNOT STAND UP TO AN ATTITUDE THAT SAYS: I WILL NOT GIVE UP! I WILL SUCCEED! I WILL WORK HARDER! I WILL NOT BE DENIED!

Neither of us ever imagined that we would some day end up with 300 employees caring for more than 1500 children! It took us a long time to reach that point, one baby step after another (no pun intended). Slowly but surely, we were figuring out how to run a childcare center. The acceleration came by us being faithful with the little that we had. We understood that our eventual victory would come as the result of thousands of small, seemingly insignificant steps. We were right—our "overnight success" would unfold over the next thirteen years!

PRINCIPLES FOR ACCELERATION

1. Prepare and begin with the end in mind.

Before you build a building, why wouldn't you calculate the costs in advance? It would be pretty embarrassing to be half finished and run out of money.

2. "See" things as they will be.

It takes belief in yourself and in what you are doing to "see" what others cannot. Put action to your words and you will be on your way!

3. Be willing to step out into the unknown.

Every great accomplishment began as a great risk. A hero is always defined by the size of his opponent—the greater the opponent, the greater the hero. Those who take the risks are the ones who reap the rewards.

4. Be faithful with the little that you have.

If you can successfully and faithfully manage little, the day will inevitably come when you can and will successfully manage a lot.

5. Don't spend what you do not have.

Debt has a way of choking the life out of your business, your marriage, and your future. If you don't have it, don't spend it—then you won't owe it!

6. Keep your word no matter what!

Those who keep their word are destined for success, while those who refuse to keep their word are destined for failure—this is true in business and in life!

7. Communicate honestly with everyone you do business with.

Communicate with everyone the same way you would like to be communicated with. You can't go wrong!

8. Don't limit your dreams to what you currently see.

Keep the window of opportunity open—you might be surprised to find that the vision that seems so big to you now is actually part of something even bigger.

CHAPTER THREE

Surviving each other

When I met Laurie, I naturally wanted to know more about her. I asked what she did. She said, "Well, I lay out by the pool."

"What do you do when you aren't laying out by the pool?" I replied.

She responded, "I go shopping."

"Ok, what do you do when you aren't at the pool or shopping?" I followed, wondering if this conversation was going anywhere.

She said, "I go out with my friends."

What I wanted to know was where she worked and what she wanted to do with her life. I eventually learned that she was studying fashion merchandising in college and was taking a lot of early childhood development classes as well. She had worked in a childcare center a few years earlier, but was fired for making too many suggestions and recommendations for change (little wonder why one of her favorite books is *If It Ain't Broke, Break It!*, by Robert J. Kriegel and Louis Patler). Her flair for design and continual pursuit of a better way to do things were talents that she would soon put to good use.

Within six months of knowing each other, we went into business together. It would be her business since I had started another job with a Fortune 150 company (one of the 150 largest companies on the NYSE). And besides, it would be a while before the childcare center would even make a profit, especially starting with only nine students. It was my responsibility to bring in enough money to cover our expenses as newlyweds and to provide additional working capital for our new business.

I could work hard and make ends meet but, to be honest, I was a little worried about Laurie's transition into the business world.

FROM LAURIE'S PERSPECTIVE
WORKING FULL TIME

I went from shopping to mopping overnight. Coming from a lifestyle where I didn't have to work and could have anything I wanted, *it was quite a change!* Suddenly I was working full-time running a childcare center, mopping floors, changing diapers (sometimes up to eighty a day!), and making decisions, then working evenings and weekends to remodel the center. My footloose and fancy-free days were over!

I had never received any training on how to run a business. (When I saw that I had checks left in my checkbook, I thought there must be money to cover them!) Henry managed the finances for the center and helped do the practical things I couldn't do, but he had the easy life. He had a great job, wore a suit every day, didn't even have to work eight hours a day, drove the nicer car, and hung out with guys who could do anything they wanted.

On top of it all, I discovered that I was pregnant! I can tell you, being pregnant and working twelve-hour days in a crummy little childcare center with virtually no operating capital, countless cockroaches, too many pressures, and the heat of the summer *was no picnic!* But it was what I chose to do, so I threw myself into it.

LIFE IN THE FAST LANE

Business and marriage would be inseparable in our lives and I believed we could make it work, but first things were first. We had a lot of work to do to get the childcare center fixed so that it would have what Laurie was promising the parents their children would be able to enjoy. Everything I made from my job we poured back into the business. (It wasn't until our second center that we even began to see any profits, and that was four years away!) We spent countless hours painting, cleaning, landscaping, etc.

At my job I applied myself and moved up to the top 2 percent of the nation in sales within the company. I then moved into management and was earning a good-sized income, big enough, I convinced Laurie, that I could get the car of my dreams: a black Porsche 911 with a turbo-tail. I would park it sideways in the parking spaces I would win in various sales contests, making quite the statement to my co-workers. It was good for my ego, but that was about it.

The Porsche and the money were new to me because I had never made that much money before. I was enjoying the high life that I only dreamed about and started to spend more time with my business friends. Most of them lived a carefree life and didn't have the weights and concerns that I had at home.

On a personal level, I was in my own little world. I knew I was not being the responsible husband and father that I needed to be, but this was a whole lot more fun than coming home to a cramped house, a business that required all my money and time, and a wife who constantly needed something. Everywhere I turned, responsibility was staring me in the face. To say the least, I was finding marriage to be a little too confining.

FROM LAURIE'S PERSPECTIVE
UNHAPPILY MARRIED

Henry could escape from my little childcare world, but I could not. I had the responsibility and couldn't leave it. What's more, my grandmother, who truly believed in me and my dream of owning a great childcare center, had backed our loan. I was not going to let her down! That was the motivating force that kept me there and kept me diligent. (The first check every month was to that loan payment.)

But my desire to please my grandmother did nothing to solve the turmoil we were going through in our marriage. Henry's attitude reached new heights when he bought his black Porsche. The fact that his car cost more than our home didn't seem to faze him. Every time I would vent my frustrations to his mother, she would say, "Hang in there, Honey, Henry will come around."

I couldn't take it any more. I deserved better than this. I wanted more than an unhappy marriage—I had a bigger vision than that. People used to call us the "perfect couple" or "Ken and Barbie," but what they saw on the outside was not what was on the inside. We had reached the bottom of the bottom where there was nothing but constant conflict.

One day Henry's mom, after she agreed that I was right and that Henry was at fault, said, "All I can say is to turn it all over to God and put it in His hands." I had never "given" such a big thing to God, but I had tried everything else I knew. I was at the end of my rope and getting the sense that Henry didn't even want to be married.

"Ok, God," I said out of desperation, "it's in Your hands." In the back of my mind I was thinking, "If this doesn't work, I'll move on. I refuse to live like this." So I went back to my little childcare world and got so busy with everyday concerns. I guess I got so busy that I finally gave God enough time to work it out—this time the way He wanted.

BREAKTHROUGH!

If I were to stop and think, which I didn't have time to do very often, I would have had to admit that my pursuit and love of money was costing me my relationship with my wife and having a negative effect on my family, my health, and my peace. There had to be a better way, but I certainly wasn't finding it.

About that time I won a weeklong vacation to Hawaii for my efforts in sales. A few days before the families were to arrive in Hawaii, all the salespeople within the company were being wined and dined and congratulated for their sales performance. In all the excitement and talk about making more money and greater opportunities, I found myself wanting to spend time alone.

I wasn't blind to the tension that had been building in our marriage and I knew it wasn't Laurie's fault. She was just trying to survive as a teacher, manager, business owner, school bus driver, and mother. It certainly wasn't my son Zachry's fault either. That only left one person to blame: me.

THINK HOW GRATEFUL YOU WOULD BE IF YOU LOST EVERYTHING YOU HAD. . . AND THEN SUDDENLY GOT IT ALL BACK AGAIN.

A day or two before Laurie arrived in Hawaii, I was relaxing and thinking of my predicament when something clicked in my heart and mind. I suddenly realized what I stood to lose as a result of what I was doing. The thought of losing my wife and son made me re-evaluate my life. To put it simply, my bubble popped! I did not want what the rest of my business friends had: broken families, multiple short-term relationships, drugs, alcohol, and strife. The honest truth is that most of my coworkers had less than perfect lives, bad marriages, and sad futures. I wanted more than that.

I no longer wanted to be part of the executive scene that I was experiencing—it was meaningless. I was feeling a gentle nudge to go another direction. I couldn't help but remember something my dad had taught me when I was as a boy: "What does it profit a man if he gains the world but loses his soul?" Was I losing my soul? I don't know, but I was about to lose my wife and family and *that was scary enough!*

29

I chose immediately to change my priorities, placing Laurie and my family above my work and my wants. Somehow, someway, God was answering Laurie's prayer. Oddly enough, what God was saying to my heart made perfect sense! It was me who was responsible for messing up our lives with my unquenchable thirst for things that were far less important than Laurie or Zachry. Perhaps following His way of doing things would bring the answers I had been looking for all along.

When Laurie arrived in Hawaii, she noticed that something had changed. We talked for hours—and things have never been the same since! I was finding that there was a better way, a way that brought balance to every area of my life. It wasn't just money or all about me anymore. What's more, having my wife forgive me for how I had acted in the past was nothing short of a miracle in itself!

LEARNING HOW TO WORK TOGETHER

I continued to work at my job, but now my vision was in line with Laurie's—we were finally working together as a team. Things did not click immediately into place, but they were beginning to come together.

In our childcare business, I took a more active role, allowing her to focus on her areas of expertise. My most important job, however, was that of a supporter and a believer in her. She had an incredible vision for the childcare center that I could easily and happily support (I had never taken the time to really see what she was doing).

The more we worked together, we learned we couldn't cross over into each other's responsibilities. We refused to make big decisions alone, even if we were the one responsible. In the evenings we would get together and discuss any big decisions and ultimately come to an agreement. It wasn't just mine or just hers—*it was ours!* This helped us stay on the same page and work in harmony.

We also discovered that talking business all the time was not very conducive to a happy marriage. There are times and places to talk business and times and places to leave it alone. On the phone, for example, I used to call throughout the day to see how she was doing and she would say, "Don't forget to buy this for the school" or "I need you to do something for me" or "Let me tell you about all these problems." It got to a point where I would avoid calling her because there was always something wrong or something needed at the business. We finally learned that when we talked throughout the day, excluding emergencies, it was to be about pleasant things, about us! Then at home she would give me a written list of things I needed to buy, fix, or know about. This kept us from trying to avoid each other because of all the negative confrontations. It worked! We then started looking forward to talking to each other and being together more often.

In our marriage, we have come to see that we have our differences, but that's ok. If we were the same, one of us wouldn't be necessary. We have learned that we communicate differently: I want to fix things while she just wants me to listen. It took me a few years to figure this out, but we can now communicate without walking away with more problems than we met to discuss.

We also learned to resolve our arguments before we went to bed. Whoever said, "Don't let the sun go down on your wrath," knew what he was talking about! Sometimes we stop and think, "What are we arguing about?" After we realize that an issue just isn't that important, we both walk away and leave it alone. It takes Laurie a little longer to forget about things than it does for me, but we have both learned to drop what is not that important.

5 TIPS FOR
WORKING TOGETHER IN BUSINESS:

1. DECIDE THAT WHERE THERE IS A WILL, THERE IS A WAY.
2. BE WILLING TO COMPROMISE TO REACH A HAPPY MEDIUM.
3. ALWAYS REMEMBER THAT YOUR SPOUSE IS NOT YOUR PROBLEM.
4. WORK AS A TEAM AND COVER EACH OTHER'S BACK.
5. DON'T TRY TO CARRY THE OTHER PERSON'S UNRESOLVED ISSUES.

It took some time for us (me, primarily) to get on the same page in regards to our marriage, our communication, and our business. The good news is that we figured it out! We were now settling into our own unique gifts that would go on to ultimately serve our purpose in life. Yes, we may get tired of each other after working closely for a while and may need a break, but that is only natural. We resolved that no matter what might happen, we would always stay married because we would not let anything or anyone come between us. We went so far as to agree that the word "divorce" would never be used in our family.

It was not long after my personal breakthrough that I remembered something else I had learned as a boy: "If a house is divided against itself, that house cannot stand" and "a double minded man is unstable in all his ways." I knew this applied to our marriage, but instead of scaring me, it excited me! I no longer wondered if God was up to something, I knew He was! My heart was changing, and I didn't mind.

The destiny we had as a family was coming more into focus and our future together was looking brighter by the day. Our foundation was set. We were unmovable. We were ready to take on the world...together.

PRINCIPLES FOR ACCELERATION

1. Don't chase money.

Money is necessary, useful, and good to have, but you cannot buy love, peace, happiness, joy, friends, or a good marriage with it. Money is NOT the root of all evil; the love of money is. Put your priorities in order with God first and there is a way to have it all!

2. Stick with your priorities.

You will always do what you want to do—so keep your priorities in proper order and in front of you at all times. Stay focused!

3. Make your marriage unbreakable.

Decide that nothing will come between you and your spouse. Then live each day with that reality in mind. A house divided against itself cannot stand.

4. Make decisions together.

Those who work together must make decisions together. It is one of the best ways to bond (or break) a working relationship. Don't allow your relationship to be played from the middle by other people. Communicate!

5. Resolve arguments quickly.

Instead of letting the chasm widen, make it a point to resolve an argument as quickly as possible. Don't go to bed mad—you will sleep much better!

6. Learn to really listen to your spouse.

Learn to listen as you would like to be listened to. You might discover something you never knew before—about yourself!

7. Don't rush God.

If you "give" a difficult issue to God, let Him work it out His way. Don't rush Him! He is the best at what He does. You are the only one who can get in your way!

CATCHING THE VISION

We hadn't been back from Hawaii very long when Laurie's often repeated phrase "I think we are on to something here" finally sank in. Was there really that much potential in a little old childcare center? I had been in more of a survival mode, working from paycheck to paycheck just to pay the bills. Our family was growing and the business continually needed capital. Now, with my new mindset, I took the time to listen and began to pay more attention to her vision and to the business possibilities she kept mentioning.

This process took a long time, but we realized later that it was all in perfect timing. I was now able to use many things that I had learned while working for a Fortune 150 corporation, scale them down and apply them in our own business. Laurie never gave me a "what-took-you-so-long?" speech. Her enthusiasm about the possibilities was contagious, but what struck me the most was that Laurie had been telling parents about her vision for the childcare center for months.

The result? The center was operating at maximum capacity *with a waiting list!* It was time to expand.

FROM LAURIE'S PERSPECTIVE
IT TAKES TWO TO TANGO

When we first started, there was no structure. I would accept whatever the parents were willing to pay me to take care of their children. Henry helped by setting price guidelines and implementing structure.

Over time the business improved and I started telling Henry, "I think we are on to something here." Even though it took him a while to catch the vision for what I was doing, I know I could not have done half of what we did if I tried to do it alone. I needed him and he needed me. I'm just thankful we figured this out when we did! Once we were in agreement, our destiny seemed to come into focus.

EXPANDING THE VISION

We decided that the best way to allow room for the ever-enlarging enrollment would be to expand the existing center. Unfortunately, we had little collateral, if any, to get another loan with. Amazingly enough, a banker was able to work with us on a government-backed loan so that we could build the expansion.

Before the doors even opened we were full! Now we were up to eighty-seven students and still having to turn people away. The parents had caught Laurie's vision for the center and for their children and were, in Laurie's words, "coming in droves!"

When I saw how quickly it filled up, I began to envision a second childcare center. Laurie, on the other hand, wanted only one center—to stay there, to make it work, and then retire in thirty or forty years. She didn't want to let go of what was comfortable and, understandably, didn't want to increase her workload, especially now that she was pregnant with our second child, Olivia. After hours of discussing the possibilities, we decided we would pursue the second childcare center.

To prepare for the new building, we visited thirty to forty different schools, asking questions and getting ideas. I was surprised how the knowledge we gained from the industry fit so well with the ideas that came to us as we worked together. Her ideas were incredible! Her floor plan is still the best in the industry and her pride and joy, a cement tricycle path around the outside play area, one of the first things she wanted, she now could have. I had Laurie list all of the other things she wanted in her version of the "perfect" childcare center. We were well on our way to putting our vision in writing for our second childcare center!

As our vision took shape, we started through the steps of looking for a piece of property, making phone calls, finding out prices, etc. We looked for property for months and still didn't find anything, but we kept looking. Then one day we finally found a piece of property in our price range. After a few weeks of negotiating, we agreed on the price and were able to purchase the empty lot. The timing and the location turned out to be perfect!

We had continued looking for that piece of property even when it seemed we would never find something we could afford, located in a good area for a childcare center. We knew the principle, "You always find what you are looking for if you keep at it long enough," and we proved it true. I know people who for years and years say, "I want to build my dream home," but they never go looking for property or never take the first small steps necessary to even start the process. Without taking the initial small steps, there is no way they are ever going to realize their dream.

SIMPLE SECRET TO SUCCESS: WRITE YOUR VISION DOWN, THEN TAKE THE CONSISTENT, NECESSARY STEPS TO GET THERE—DON'T GIVE UP!

Now that we found our ideal property, our next challenge would be getting another loan. We had barely been approved for a loan to expand our first childcare center, but this would be a larger building and would require a much larger loan. I went to seven bankers and they all rejected me!

I went home and regrouped. When I approached the eighth banker, he immediately said the prospects did not look good (I knew what that meant!). I said, "Please don't tell me I can't get the loan. Tell me what I need to do so that I can get the loan. Give me a list of things I need to do and I'll do them." I asked him if he would drive to the property with me so I could show him our vision. To my surprise he agreed.

He got in my car and we drove to see the site. He then proceeded to tell me what I would need to do to secure the loan. The list was long and the paperwork was like writing a thesis, but we moved forward. Since we had no money to hire someone to fill out all of the paperwork necessary to apply for an S.B.A. loan, I did it myself. Still working for another company to help make ends meet, the time constraints were almost unbearable. However, we did it! Within a few weeks, which seemed like years, we received our approval and the new construction was underway. Oddly enough, it was this same banker who initially turned us down for our loan who later nominated us for the S.B.A. entrepreneur of the year award. We went on to the win that award for a five-state region.

The second childcare center was everything Laurie envisioned it to be, but within ninety days of opening its doors, we were already full! We needed to expand again!

I sat down with Laurie and discussed our options. By this time she knew what we ought to do, even if she didn't necessarily like it. Sadly, her cement tricycle path was right where the expansion would need to go.

We were beginning to grow and our reputation was beginning to build. Our main focus was simply doing what we told people we would do. Simple as it sounds, the parents and children loved us! This was all good for business, but Laurie was still doing most of the everyday work at the childcare center, while I continued to work full time at my job, I knew a fresh goal would help push her forward, so I made a proposal: if we expanded the second childcare center and it filled, we could build a new house.

The two-bedroom house we lived in was no longer adequate for our growing family. Our three children were crammed in one bedroom with no closets! It also happened to be right next door to our first center, which gave us no privacy. Anytime we did anything out of the usual or, heaven forbid we get a new car (even a used one that was new to us), the parents would make comments like, "We know who's paying for that!"

We were consumed with running the business, but the timing seemed right to expand. Laurie agreed and we went ahead with the second expansion and it filled immediately as well.

FROM LAURIE'S PERSPECTIVE
LETTING GO OF THE COMFORTABLE

Let's face it—we like to be comfortable. It's human nature. When Henry said we should build a second center, I couldn't believe it. Here I was working myself to death with one center and he wanted me to take on another center? Forget it!

He wisely took the time to explain how the first step of multiplication is always the most difficult, how a new building would not have any cockroaches or need any repairs, and through delegating I could actually decrease my workload. Before, we did not have the revenues to hire anyone to delegate to! But this new plan, assuming we could attract children to the center, would include the appropriations of money for the help we needed. I saw the logic and potential and came into agreement with Henry. I caught his vision!

I admit, Henry had to push me a little bit to get into the second center. (I even struggled when I had to get a new checking account—that account represented the beginning of a dream that was coming true in our life and I didn't want to change!) The whole process of a second center was a big step for me, but once we did it, I started to see how we could do it again and again. It also felt great to be able to work together.

FURTHER CHANGES IN THE WIND

The more I got involved with the childcare centers and Laurie's vision, the less I enjoyed going to my job each day. In fact, I began to hate my once perfect job. I was at the top and was doing well financially, but my interest in the business side of what Laurie was doing was nothing short of intense. What was happening to me? The growth, banking, loans, building, projecting finances, setting up goals and targets for the employees to attain, etc. were capturing my heart and mind.

> # THE TRICK TO DELEGATING IS GETTING PEOPLE TO UNDERSTAND YOUR VISION.
> –LAURIE PENIX

All of these new desires came *after* my personal breakthrough in Hawaii. I knew what that meant—God was making things happen on our behalf. Getting the loans was unexplainable, but the speed in which the centers filled up was nothing short of miraculous.

What was I doing differently that caused the change? I realized that instead of chasing after money first, I was pursuing God's will first, which meant I was starting to line my life up with His Word (obeying the Bible and obeying what I sensed He was telling me to do). As a result, I was becoming the responsible husband that I needed to be. My priorities also lined up and were placed in their proper order. All of the sudden it wasn't all about me anymore. How else could I explain how every area of my life was being positively affected? Things were beginning to run faster and smoother than I had ever imagined.

At this point, after more than four years in the business and with the second childcare center expansion full, we started making a profit that equaled what I had been bringing home from my job. All sorts of questions went through my mind, the primary one being: should I quit my job and work in the childcare business full-time? If this was indeed my destiny, I reasoned with myself, then I needed to pursue it.

It took me six months to write my letter of resignation. When I finally submitted it, I was both relieved and afraid at the same time. The day after I resigned, with no insurance, no benefits, no perks, nothing, Laurie told me that she was pregnant with our third child—Madison!

I lost all my security in one fell swoop. However, I did have a peace in my heart like never before that I was doing the right thing. It was a step of faith for me as well, even though I had been the one encouraging Laurie to step out of her comfort zone and dream bigger dreams. When we made the decision for both of us to go full-time in the childcare business, we never looked back.

Principles for Acceleration

1. Sell your vision.

Sell your vision until the right people buy it who can help you achieve it. At that point, your job will be much easier. People die without a vision; mentally, emotionally, and sometimes physically.

2. Knowledge without wisdom is useless.

You have to mix the two together. When we take what we learn and add that to God's wisdom that He gives us, we can expect the extraordinary!

3. Take the first step toward multiplication.

Taking the first step is the hardest part of multiplication and increase, but once you get the ball rolling, it builds momentum and gets easier by the day.

4. See it, then take action.

Walk toward your dreams. It is not enough to have the dream, you must take the necessary practical steps toward making it into a reality, day by day.

5. Set goals as you need them.

Along the way, set specific short-term goals and personal rewards for achieving those goals. This will motivate, encourage, and keep you going. It will also add more fuel to your fire—making you burn longer with stronger passion.

6. Step out of your comfort zone.

*Don't be afraid to step out of your comfort zone—
the place that you feel secure or comfortable. Do
it today. Tomorrow you will say, "I wish I had
done it earlier." To get what you've never had,
you must do what you've never done.*

7. Pursue peace.

*You cannot buy peace. When you have peace in
your heart that you are where you need to be and
doing the right thing, don't trade that peace for
anything, not even money!*

CHAPTER FIVE

TOTAL COMMITMENT— NO LOOKING BACK!

The more time I spent working with Laurie on the child-care centers, the more I became aware that it was not my wisdom or experience that was leading the way, and neither was it Laurie's. There was no other way we could explain it—God must be directing our steps. After doing my own thing for so many years, I was a little surprised that God would care that much about me to take such an active role in our lives. I learned He does that with everyone if we let Him, but I was still discovering God's love for me. The fact that He would have great plans for my life was overwhelming!

Whenever we were faced with an important decision or a seemingly big opportunity, I would say, "God, I'm going to take the steps toward this and if it is not of you, please close the door in such a way that I can't open it." (It is my nature to push and push to open something, but if God closes it, then I know I'll never get it open.)

I guess you could say we were beginning to have more of a personal relationship with God. We knew He was in control and that He had bigger plans for our lives than either of us realized, but we were not sure what role we played in the relationship. It was God who had the big plans and saw the big picture; our job was to walk it out. Part of that, we recognized, would mean being increasingly obedient to what He said, whether to us directly, through circumstances, or through His written Word.

We also started to go to church and tithe (we had always helped other people with our time and money, but had never tithed before). It didn't take much to see the momentum that was building in our business, but it was also building in our personal and spiritual lives as well.

LOOK BEFORE YOU LEAP

When the expansion to the second childcare center filled, we started the process of preparing to build a home, a first for us, one that would actually fit our family! By this time Madison had arrived, which meant three children under the age of six were crammed in one small bedroom in a two-bedroom, 1400 square-foot home.

Just as we did with our second childcare center, we started out by writing down our vision. We then began looking for a place to build. It was a pretty big move for us, going into a house three times the size of our current one and in a very nice neighborhood. We had done our best to prepare financially for my shift to working full-time in the childcare business and for us building a new home. However, fear and doubt seemed to lurk in the shadows. One afternoon I remember calling my mother and asking her to save a little back for us each month "just in case this doesn't work out." This move was a big step of faith for both of us.

We had been faithful with the little money our centers made. Instead of spending our money on something frivolous, we kept reinvesting the money back into the business. As the business grew we found ourselves in a position to build a new home. We weren't really sure what size of a home we would qualify for but we were going to go for our dream. I found myself making a bigger deal about the costs involved than it was worth. I was almost losing the joy of the moment in my search for the perfect location to build. I had plot plans for three different locations and they all looked good. This made the process of selecting the perfect one very difficult because I kept analyzing and re-analyzing each location. One day as I was driving around looking for a lot to build on, I prayed, "God, where would be the perfect place to build?" He asked, "Where do you want to build?" When I answered, He then said, "OK, now start taking the necessary steps to do it." In essence, "Relax and get to work." So I did.

I was learning how to walk in balance and wasn't so driven to be "perfect." Part of that balance, I realized, meant being financially conservative. I would figure out on paper the possibilities before we leapt into something big. I felt it was my responsibility to do so. However, it seemed that everything we "went for" was always just beyond our grasp. I guess that's what faith is—taking the steps towards something that you could never do on your own and then giving the glory to God for your successes. What a great way to do things!

Building a new home was cutting it closer than we had intended, but we both were in agreement about it. It was a step of faith, but not our first. Each time we had pushed the envelope and walked towards something bigger than we thought we could handle, God showed up and we would make it! Why should this be any different?

We had been faithful with the little we had and we did our best to walk in balance—not in excess. We recognized that to get where we wanted to go, we had to try and do things right from day one. We always paid people what we owed, we treated those around us like we would want to be treated, we were current on all of our taxes, and we actually did what we said we would do. We planned big. Most people laughed and thought we were crazy, but when it came time to do some of the things we had planned to do, we had the confidence that it would be successful—and by now we had learned to always give God the glory.

What's more, much to Laurie's delight, I felt it was time to get rid of my black Porsche 911. I was letting go of a piece of my image because I knew there was something better for me. My priorities were now beginning to line up in proper order.

FROM LAURIE'S PERSPECTIVE
TAKING CARE OF THE REAL BUSINESS

Teachers and managers were the ones who make every childcare center work. I understood that from day one, so when parents thanked me for what we were doing for their children, I would say, "Thank you, I appreciate that, but please thank the teachers because they are the ones who do all the work."

In an industry where turnover is 50 to 60 percent, I made it a point to value each helper, teacher, and director. Each year we gave our employees year-end bonuses, Christmas parities, went on retreats and trips together, provided insurance, and more. We always tried to take care of the people who took care of our business. As a result, growth and positive attitudes increased.

WRONG, BUT UNEXPECTEDLY RIGHT

If the first and second childcare centers filled so quickly, it only seemed logical that a third center would fill as well. I found a piece of property that was ideally situated for our third center. The loan was already approved and we had prayed our customary "God, close the door if it isn't of you" prayer, but I kept pressing forward with the deal, despite the fact that we both didn't feel 100 percent right about it. The lack of peace was the closed door, but I wasn't willing to let it go. Then, just days before we were to close, I became very sick and started to cough up blood. I ended up in the hospital for five days with pneumonia.

Laurie was willing to try to do the closing without me, but circumstances of the deal required that I be there or there would be no deal. I was flat on my back in the hospital and obviously couldn't be there, but the finality of the "no" gave both of us a sense of relief. I used those five days to think and reconsider my actions. I had no question that God was blessing the work of our hands, but I realized that I was impatiently trying to go make something happen too hard. My life was not in balance. I had put the "deal" in front of everything else, including my health. Scripture says that the Holy Spirit will lead, guide, and teach us in all things. In short, to succeed, all I need to do is take the first step to put myself in motion by walking towards my goal. And at the same time, submit my life to the leading, guiding and teaching of the Holy Spirit. That way I am not getting in my own way! I could do that—and it would be much less stressful.

WHEN YOU UNITE TWO DIVERSE STRENGTHS, YOU HAVE A DANGEROUS COMBINATION—NOTHING CAN WITHSTAND IT! SUCH IS THE POWER OF A HUSBAND AND WIFE COMING INTO AGREEMENT.

Amazingly enough, when I walked out of the hospital, I was totally healed, and never coughed again! Our family was able to go on a skiing vacation we had promised our children, just three weeks later. We then went back to focusing on our two centers and new home that was under construction. We ultimately finished our new home and moved in. At 4,000+ square feet, we couldn't believe our eyes. We were wondering how we would ever fill all the closets, coming from a home that barely had closets. Financing of the home worked out good as well. I had a reputation for always financing things at the maximum terms, giving myself room if I needed it, but with no pre-payment penalties. In just seven years, we were able to pay off our entire mortgage! God is good!

It was around this time that I was nominated for the S.B.A. Entrepreneur of the Year award. Because of it, bankers were coming out of the woodwork, offering us loans without us even having to ask! The award was like an official seal of approval that proved valuable whenever we dealt with banks.

Soon after, another childcare center came up for sale. It was a high dollar spot, but the building came nowhere near our standards of excellence. When we stopped by to look at it, we were given an outrageous price for it. We understood the potential in the little building, but we politely declined and walked away. I had learned my lesson in the hospital bed: don't push too hard it if it isn't God!

A couple months later the owners called us at home on a Tuesday night and said, "If you can have the money to us by Friday, you can have it." Their asking price was much less than we had originally offered just a few months previous! It was an incredible deal, but getting a loan of that size usually takes a minimum of forty-five to sixty days.

Fortunately, we were still pre-approved for the loan on the property that we could not buy because of my sickness. As a result, we had the money by Friday afternoon and were in our third center before we even realized it. God used my mistake with pursuing the wrong center to help us with this new center. I have learned in life that God will never use your past to condemn you, but instead cause your past to bow down and serve your future in Him! How good is that?

The eyesore of a building had been a childcare center for seventeen years, but one night Laurie had a dream of what the center could look like if remodeled. I had an architect draw it up and we were able to complete the remodeling without closing the doors once! The finished product was magnificent, "adorable" as Laurie says, and it made a big impact in that community and in the city for our Koala Care centers. It filled faster the first month than it had ever filled in the history of that center! Momentum continued to build.

FROM LAURIE'S PERSPECTIVE
BELIEVE YOU CAN DO IT

People have always told me I couldn't do this or shouldn't do that. They didn't speak encouraging words toward me. I learned that most friends don't want to see you succeed. They are quick to give you their opinion or view with hopes that you will abandon your goal.

I have also learned that I have to focus on my goal, even if I'm not 100 percent certain, because if I don't focus, someone will come in and try to sabotage my dream. If I let what they say sway me too much, my goal gets out of focus.

Instead, I choose to believe that I can do whatever it is I am aiming for. If I'm not sure the vision I have is from God, I walk toward it. If I continue to overcome the obstacles along the way, then I know I will eventually succeed.

PUSHING THE BOUNDARIES

We had spied a piece of property on the outskirts of town that we thought would make an ideal location for a fourth child-care center. The property had been pastureland for 50-60 years and was selling for pennies on the dollar, but nobody had bought it. The reason was there was no sewer to use and the soil would not perk for a septic system (the soil would not absorb the septic runoff fast enough to be approved for anything but pasture land). This meant that the only way to build a building would be for the ground to perk or for a sewer system to exist, but neither option was available.

The town was moving in this direction and I liked the property and saw its potential, but I was at a stalemate. Everyone else had passed over this prime piece of real estate for the same reason. On the other side of the road was a large assisted living facility and I thought, "They must have a sewer system, since the ground is the same on both sides of the road."

So I asked around and found that the original architect who designed the assisted living facility many years ago was still alive and in the area. When I met with him, I was amazed to discover that he still had the plans for the building and the utility layout that the city didn't even have. It turns out there was a dedicated sewer line that came up just across the road from the property I wanted to buy! I quickly got approval from the people next door to go through their property and hook up to the sewer line on the condition that I would hook them up for free. We turned a $60,000 piece of property into a much more valuable piece of property almost overnight!

We quickly secured a loan and began construction. A few local people asked what we were doing and how big the childcare center was going to be. They happened to have their own childcare center in the area and said, "We've had our center of fifty kids for fifteen years now and you want to put one in for 160 kids? There is no way you will ever succeed!"

What we didn't tell them was that we would have to charge nearly 30 percent more than they did just to make it work! Instead of basing our decision on what they had to say, we continued on in the process. I had checked on the population growth, talked to some people in the area about business, and most importantly, my wife and I were in agreement and we both had peace. We knew it would work.

To stop what we were doing at that moment would have been giving in to the fear of failure. As my father says, "Fear, when broken down to its core elements, is nothing more than F.E.A.R.— False Evidence Appearing Real." We chose to step forward in faith rather than be pulled back out of fear. We knew we couldn't be double minded, trying to hold onto fear and faith at the same time. We chose to let go of fear and grasp with faith the future that we believed was ours. We believed God was directing our steps, which meant that any and all fear was unfounded.

The building went up on schedule and filled with children in a few months. In addition, the remaining property that we bought but did not use for the childcare center increased in value to the point where it was worth more than the entire center we had just put in!

Business was continuing to pick up speed.

PRINCIPLES FOR ACCELERATION

1. Say "no" to fear.

Fear is nothing more than False Evidence Appearing Real (F.E.A.R.). Don't listen to it! You can only hold on to faith or fear, not both.

2. Take care of your people.

The more you show your appreciation for your employees, the better they will perform, and the more you show your appreciation for them, the better they will perform, and the more you...

3. Play it safe and do what it takes.

Most businesses fail within the first two years due to financial problems. Being conservative now will more than pay for itself in the end!

4. Don't be afraid to walk away.

Not every great opportunity is as great as it might appear. For whatever the reason, if you don't have peace about something, don't do it. Success is never in a hurry, but we are.

5. Dream BIG.

You will spend the same amount of time in any given day working on your dream, big or small. Choose BIG.

6. Believe you CAN do it.

Begin with the premise that you CAN do it and then focus on your goal. Don't listen to the

56

"advice" (discouraging words) of your friends—your faith is not in them anyway.

7. Don't take "no" for an answer.

If you are pursuing your dreams and you know God has opened the door, then keep going. The answer you seek will eventually come.

8. Get in motion.

It is much easier to move an object in motion than it is to move a stationary object. The same law of physics applies to you and the Holy Spirit; He leads, but nothing can be led unless it is first in motion.

CHAPTER SIX

GROWTH IN THE
MIDST OF SETBACKS

Business was indeed growing, but not without its fair share of bumps and setbacks. Just as we were about to open our fourth location, two of our best-trained managers suddenly quit. Laurie was devastated. It had taken her years to train them and one of them was weeks away from being given Laurie's responsibilities, so I could understand her hurt and disappointment. Instead of getting a much-needed break, Laurie had to work even harder.

We knew it would require years to train another person to take Laurie's position, but we also knew we had to start looking for that key person within the employees we already had or would soon hire. In the meantime, we threw ourselves into managing our four childcare centers, all operating at maximum capacity.

FROM LAURIE'S PERSPECTIVE
DEALING WITH SETBACKS

It hurt terribly for me to lose my support staff, but I couldn't change anything. Henry had said in one of our staff meetings, "My prayer is that those people who are supposed to be here will be with us to build the company, and those who shouldn't will be gone."

Within two weeks, two key managers left! We didn't make them leave; they just quit one day. I was sad and overwhelmed, but I was not complaining. I figured God had a reason for it all—I would buckle down and continue to do my part to the best of my ability.

GREATER GROWTH THROUGH ADVERSITY

In addition to looking for top managers, I kept looking for property that would be ideally suited for a new childcare center, location five. We both recognized it made good business sense to get another center going, but physically speaking, we felt maxed out. We decided to proceed, slowly, and see if God would open the doors.

I had found a vacant lot in front of a very nice neighborhood. It would be perfect, so I submitted a contract on the new location, subject to us receiving adequate zoning to accept a childcare center. Zoning was a constant challenge, but I had always received favor in front of the zoning board. Our reputation was growing as people who actually did what they said they were going to do; this was a very important part of our ultimate success.

As the zoning procedures continued, we discovered that many of the neighbors were in opposition to our building. We immediately set up a meeting with president of the homeowners association. The meeting was to be held in the school cafeteria that was right next door to the empty lot we wanted. When I arrived, there were 123 angry homeowners there as well! "Who do you think you are?" they demanded. "We are not going to have a daycare built in the front entrance to our neighborhood!" They were not very happy with the prospects, to say the least.

They were also not familiar with how we did business or the quality we projected. From their perspective, and I couldn't blame them, they probably envisioned a cheap-looking daycare center at the entrance of their neighborhood that would not only be an eyesore, but would decrease their property value as well.

When the meeting began, I stood up in a this-is-what-we-*are-doing* attitude (instead of a this-is-what-we-are-*trying-to-do* attitude) and handed out an architectural rendition of our vision. I then, very politely, answered any questions that they had.

After we battled through that meeting, we then went to the zoning board meeting. It had to be stopped twice to quiet the people down. They were so irate that everyone thought we were crazy for even pursuing the idea. With God's help, I maintained an attitude of peace and certainty and kept pursuing it. We believed we were doing the right thing and continued to meet with the homeowners association and zoning board. After three months of discussions, it was approved! It came down to a list of what the president of the homeowners association wanted and what we wanted. When we compared lists, they were nearly identical. We were on our way to building our fifth location!

When the childcare center was completed, many of the neighbors came to us and said, "Thank you for putting this in." The center was beautiful—all brick with white columns and a covered driveway to drop off the children. It was as nice as some of the homes in the neighborhood. Again, we did what we said we would do and did it with excellence. It felt good to hear their positive comments, but we felt we should take one more step toward reconciling a previously volatile situation: we waived the enrollment fee for any of the homeowners who wished to enroll their children. Acting out of love was simply the right thing to do.

PERSONAL GROWTH BEFORE BUSINESS GROWTH

I believe that long-term growth in business must be preceded by personal growth. I consider this to be character growth in any area of life, whether it's financial, mental, emotional, physical, or spiritual. Short-term business growth is often easy to come by, but for growth to be maintained and/or for that individual to maintain all that he or she has gained, personal growth is required. This principle applies to everyone, myself included.

While we were preparing to open our newest location, center five, we had heard of a local church that needed financial support to expand their childcare center. In essence, they were competition, but we felt we should give toward their vision. We wrote them a sizeable check, even though we needed the money for ourselves as we were hiring more staff, paying for new supplies, and marketing the new center, not to mention the new loan for the building and property. At the same time we started regularly giving and tithing 10 percent or more of our income to our local church and various ministries that were feeding us spiritually.

The night of the grand opening of our newest center, which was licensed for 217 children, we logged in over 800 people who wanted a tour or to sign-up! We were almost full the day we opened. What a miracle!

I believe the business success we were experiencing came as a result of the personal growth that had already taken place in many different areas of our lives. We had made progress:

◈ Our marriage was steady
◈ I had stopped drinking completely (one or two drinks used to turn into ten)
◈ We were working together as a team
◈ We were good stewards over what God had given us
◈ We were tithing regularly
◈ We were stepping out in faith
◈ We were walking in what we believed to be the will of God

We had many areas that we were still working on, but whenever we would see something that needed improvement, we would focus on that. I am thankful that God didn't require us to be perfect before He could bless us. If that were the case, we would have never been blessed. It turns out that our progress was getting the attention of other childcare centers as well. An executive of a national childcare company flew to town with an architect to try to copy what we were doing. Thankfully, one of the employees recognized them and wouldn't let them in the building. Other competing companies would send their managers by to snoop on us. After literally having to fight off spies, Laurie said one day, "This is getting crazy, in a good way!"

She was the one primarily responsible for breaking the mold of what a childcare center "should" be. Her vision was radically different, but like bees to honey, our phenomenal success kept the "spies" coming.

Professionals who had been in the business for years or had even written books on childcare were saying, "You can't do it this way," but we were. My vision for the finances and computer programs to monitor financial activity fit perfectly with Laurie's vision for the programs, protocol, materials, décor, etc. We were a dangerous team! Ours was the "perfect recipe" that everyone wanted. We believed we could go anywhere with our whole plan and it would succeed.

In the midst of all this growth, an employee with tremendous potential began to emerge. Laurie was excited with the possibilities of a qualified manager taking her place. I was not so thrilled and purposefully grilled Laurie's hopeful replacement, Michelle, with difficult questions about the budgets, judgment calls, training, programs, etc. I just knew that no one could operate the centers like we did. To my amazement, she answered all of my questions like I would have answered them myself. She was one of the hardest working, most trustworthy, and faithful individuals we had ever encountered in the childcare business, or for that matter, in any other business. Within the year, Michelle (who later earned the coveted nickname "Mimi") took Laurie's place! It was a great day to finally overcome an obstacle that had been in our way for many years.

FROM LAURIE'S PERSPECTIVE
START SMALL

Individuals who ask for business advice, then ask the same endless questions of other people, are the ones who never start anything. They seem to get caught up in the process and never reach the promise. It takes work to accomplish your dreams, but those who want everything given to them or analyze a deal to death will never reach their goals.

Those who do receive advice and take the first step, their creative momentum begins to build. Soon they are taking bigger and bigger steps toward their goals. Starting small is nothing to be ashamed of, while not starting at all is a shame.

MAKING TIME FOR THE FAMILY

In the midst of getting loans, changing diapers, rezoning property, and managing people, when do you find time for the family? Laurie and I knew we wouldn't find time—we would have to **make** time.

When Laurie's expected replacement quit just before we opened our fourth center, we made the decision to have someone come in and cook dinner and help clean for us. That way we could have dinner as a family before our three children went to bed. The investment in our family was well worth it.

A few years earlier we had decided that we would take our children to school and pick them up every day, unless we were out of town or in a real bind at work. It worked and our schedules fit around our priorities. We were able to spend quality time together as a family.

When our oldest, Zachry, reached the age where he started playing soccer, I decided that I could spend more time with him if I coached the team. Again, we worked it around our busy schedules because it was important to us. We are still growing in this area and realize that the relationship that we have with our children now will directly affect their futures. A parent will have many opportunities to work on various dreams, but only one opportunity to raise a family. And in the end, like my mom always tells me, "Your family is all that matters—they will always be the ones who are there for you when everyone else gives up or leaves after getting from you what they wanted." How true!

We also used to sit down once a week (now it's about every month) and have a family meeting/Bible study where we would discuss the changes we were making. Our children watched us walk through difficult setbacks and challenges and we wanted them to learn from our experiences as well. Sometimes the results were not what we expected.

When Zachry was twelve and starting to take care of the yard, we opened a checking account for him. When I paid him his first check for doing the lawn, he immediately wrote a check for his tithe! I had never told him what he should do—but he had watched us and seen the blessings that came as a result of us tithing.

The comments that each of them makes at different times is evidence to us that the principles we are learning and things that we are experiencing are sinking into their hearts and minds as well. We are still making progress, but deciding to **make** time as a family was a pivotal moment for all of us!

ATTEMPTS TO STOP YOU BEFORE YOU START

In the middle of a setback or difficulty, it isn't always easy to see the big picture, but later when you look back it is always plain. There have been many times when we were about to experience a breakthrough or do something new that we suddenly found ourselves in a position that seemed doomed to failure. The 123 ranting homeowners, the "You can't get a loan here!" from the bankers, or the impossibility of filling up a childcare center that was already under construction were nothing but smoke screens to throw us off track. I have always said that if a vision can be destroyed, it will be destroyed in its infancy when it is weakest and most vulnerable to attack.

Laurie and I have faced challenges every step of the way. Looking back, some of them seem almost comical, but at the time, they were not so funny. When Laurie was sixteen years old, she was working in a convention center for a large ministry and was asked to "fake" a healing. That affected her view of Christianity in a negative way. Years later, when we were getting to know each other, she came to my dad's church and immediately classified me and my family as being "holy rollers," akin to the fake healers she had experienced earlier. As she began to experience God for herself and His miraculous powers, she knew He was real. Had she walked away and never spoken to me again because of her previous bad experience (or smokescreen), our destiny together would have definitely been delayed.

Even the time Laurie was fired from a childcare center while in high school was a smoke screen over her future. She changed the childcare industry only a few years later, but had she allowed discouragement to set in, she would have never allowed herself to be creative and push the boundaries of the status quo.

Several years after we built our first home, we started the process of looking for a piece of property all over again, but this time it was for a new dream home. Just as before, we wrote our vision down and began to take the first steps to obtain it. We searched for property until one day we came across a piece of land that was suitable for a neighborhood development. It was beautifully landscaped with trees and ponds and seemed to be perfect. I took the first step and began to inquire of the price and specifications. I thought with our building experience, we could buy the entire property (200+ acres), build a neighborhood, and keep a portion of the land for our dream home. Just a few weeks later we decided not to get into the home building business, but instead asked if the owners would sell us just a part of the land. To our amazement, they agreed and sold us twenty-five acres of land, surrounded by a natural creek, beautiful tall trees, and a fishpond! It was a dream come true.

The blessing continued. Only a few days after we purchased our land, it was appraised for almost double what we had originally purchased it for. Momentum was continuing to build, but not without hurdles. Significant unexpected costs came up and people began to tell us, "Do you have any idea what you are doing?" Debt was mounting and I found myself wondering again if I had made the right choice.

In the middle of construction, countless thoughts ran through my mind about running out of money and not being able to provide for my family. I remember visiting the job site where our home was being built one Friday afternoon and was so stricken with fear (another smoke screen) that I began to physically get sick. I spent the next two days in bed wondering what was happening to me. When I got out of bed on Monday morning, I felt very strongly in my spirit that I should not quit. I told the general contractor to continue working and we never looked back again.

> **WHEN THINGS "CAN'T GET ANY WORSE," THAT IS NOT THE TIME TO QUIT—THAT IS THE TIME TO KEEP GOING. SUCCESS IS RIGHT AROUND THE CORNER!**

At that moment I realized there was a choice to be made. I had to choose whether I would operate in fear and quit or operate in faith and press forward. Again, my prayer was, "God if this door is supposed to be open then help me walk through it and if it's supposed to be closed, close it so that I can't open it." The door was open and we walked through it. We completed our dream home and it has been a wonderful testimony to everyone who has visited. God's wonderful love was shown to all the sub-contractors working on the home, as I would make it a point to tell all of them the blessings that God had poured upon us for believing in Him. The end result was even better than I had imagined. We now hold Bible studies and have counseled world leaders in our new home. Relationships have been healed and many other miracles have occurred, all as a result of our believing and not giving up.

I learned that if you just hang in there and hold on to the dreams you first had, the smoke will eventually lift and you will be able to see more clearly. If you can get past the smoke, you will experience something that very few people have ever witnessed: the incredible acceleration of your destiny, which is nothing less than the good things that God has already prepared and planned that you should walk in!

Principles for Acceleration

1. Make setbacks your green light.

When setbacks slow you down, resist the urge to quit or even look down. See setbacks as a green light to press forward with increased effort.

2. Return spite with kindness.

Give the people who act spitefully toward you the benefit of the doubt and treat them with kindness. They may become your greatest allies!

3. Give out of obedience.

If you feel you should give someone (even a competitor) your time, talent, or money, then do it. Obedience to God is your ticket to accelerating your destiny.

4. See personal growth as vital.

Personal growth is the foundation for all long-term business success. It is the base on which everything else is built!

5. Make time for your family.

*You will not find the time for family; you must **make** the time. When you do, your schedule has an amazing ability to work itself around your priorities.*

6. Blow through smoke screens.

When it comes to your destiny, smoke screens are inevitable. Maintain your course and you'll blow through every one of them. Never mistake a smoke screen for a closed door; keep moving forward.

7.Walk by faith and not by sight.

*Even if things don't "appear" to be going the way you thought, know that a good idea may come to pass, but a God idea **must** come to pass!*

Principles for Acceleration

ACCELERATION!

After such a battle over rezoning the property for our fifth childcare center, our next center's (number six) two zoning meetings prior to approval seemed like a piece of cake. The property we bought was more than we needed for the new center. Soon after the center was built, it *filled to capacity*. We later discovered that the value of the extra land had increased to the point where it now was worth more than the new childcare center we built. Just like we had experienced with our fourth center!

Things were happening rapidly. It seemed like what used to take two years was now taking two months. It was incredible! In this accelerated state, you just have to hang on because the speed is dizzying!

❖ Center number six filled in less than sixty days.
❖ We found land for our dream home.
❖ We were making wiser and quicker decisions.
❖ Our key managers were right in sync with our vision.
❖ All of our childcare centers had waiting lists.
❖ Our family was blessed, vacationing together and in perfect health.
❖ We were living in our dream home and driving our dream car.
❖ We were able to give to those around us.
❖ National childcare chains were waving millions of dollars under our noses with hopes that we would join them.

By this time I was well acquainted with the fact that it wasn't me causing the acceleration—God was the one directing our steps. He deserved the credit; my job was to take the steps and implement the principles I was learning. The specific steps are different for everyone, but the principle of walking it out one step at a time, as He directs, will always remain the same.

What's more, God is not bound by time, money, or any other hindrance we might face. No matter how big or how crazy the dream might be, if we are careful to walk it out, it will come to pass! This involves the implementing of God's Word into our lives. Scripture says, *"If you abide in Me, and My words abide in you, you will ask what you desire, and it shall be done for you"* (John 15:7, NKJV). When His words are in me, I can ask for what I desire and it will come to pass! Of course, when His Word is inside of me, my desires and vision will be in line with His. I didn't think I would ever be doing it, but here I was asking for His will to be done in my life. What a concept!

In an effort to make this as real and tangible as possible, I wrote up a single-page prayer of blessing and started speaking these biblical truths over myself and my family...and one thing led to another.

THE "PENIX FAMILY BLESSINGS"

We would read our "Penix Family Blessings"[1] (See Appendix A) every day or several times a week, whether at the dinner table or on the way to school. It wasn't long before we noticed a change in our perspective and level of expectation for what God would do in our lives and in the lives of our three children.

God had showed me how *"death and life are in the power of the tongue"* (Proverbs 18:21, KJV). God created the earth by speaking it into existence and I was created in the image of God! If I was created in the image of God and what He spoke happened,

---

[1] See Appendix A for the complete "Penix Family Blessings."

did that mean that what I spoke would happen? If so, then what I speak also carries with it a degree of the co-creative power that God used when He created the world. I can speak to what is not and it will be—if I believe it and if God's Word abides in me!

This was not the name it and claim it, blab it and grab it, mentality that has so distorted the power of God's Word. Instead, it is me coming to a revelation of what God intended for my life and walking in accordance with it. Receiving what He has for me is a gift I receive, not something I "claim" or "grab."

At one of the most difficult times in our lives, where everything seemed to be piling up on top of us, we began to speak God's Word over our business and family. Believe me, this was not the time to be testing something just to see if it worked! We were accumulating more debt on our home and in our businesses than ever before, but amazingly, as we spoke God's Word through the "Penix Family Blessings," things began to change. Our dream home was being built, we went on vacations as a family, we found the right cars at the right times, we were loving each other more and more, we were walking in perfect health, our extended family was coming together, and our children were having breakthroughs at school. It was all happening at once.

I see it like this: if you have $100 million in your bank account, why would you limit yourself to only using $100? God offers us so much, yet we usually only accept a small portion of it, mainly because we don't think we are worthy or worth it. When you understand that you are "worth" the blood of Jesus—the price He paid for you—then you will know for certain that you are "worthy" to receive all of what God has already prepared for you! I wanted more of what God intended for me and for my family. The "Penix Family Blessings" we read was not just another formula for success. Instead, it was part of the overall process that God was working into our lives. *And when God works, He works wonders!*

The great thing about this is that if God did it for me, He will do it for you. His Word says that He is no respecter of persons (Acts 10:34). That means God is impartial and does not show favoritism. He is, however, a respecter of faith, meaning that He will show partiality and favoritism to those who take Him at His word and **act on it!** In Isaiah 43:26, God makes reference to putting Him in remembrance of His own words and in Hebrews 4:16 He makes reference to us coming boldly before His throne. God does not forget His own words, He simply wants us to come boldly before Him and speak those words out! The power of death and life is in your tongue. What are you speaking into your future?

FROM LAURIE'S PERSPECTIVE
MONEY ISN'T EVERYTHING

Sometimes people get way off on a money kick, but it isn't all about money. Money is important, but it is not the most important thing in life. To say, "I won't have money so I can be holy" is not right either. You can have money and be holy, and have a good family, and have peace, and be prosperous in all areas of your life. You can still have the drive for success in all areas of your life, but only when you seek God's kingdom or His way of doing things first.

The key thing that drew Henry and I back together was lining ourselves up with God and His Word. Money, sought after with the wrong motives or from an improper perspective, was one of the things that drove us apart.

BLESSING BEYOND OUR WILDEST DREAMS

While all of this was happening, we learned that two childcare centers (one 20,000 and the other 27,000-sq. ft), were going up for sale. A multi-million dollar company in town was closing and needed to sell off its assets and obtain relief from its existing leases. The buildings were licensed for about 700-800 children and were used primarily for the large employer that was going out of business. One of the buildings had been renovated with over $3 million worth of work and equipment, while the other had recently added a large new commercial kitchen.

We began the process again. We took the first step and inquired of the price and specifications. They called us back, thinking we were the Koala Bear Care changing station company (with deep pockets) and asked us to bid on the buildings. They were trying to get a good price for the combined $3 million worth of renovations, supplies, and equipment in their facilities. The two centers would almost double our total number of children in the other six centers, so I quickly put together and submitted a proposal. Whenever I would pray about the facilities, the verse *"The Lord your God will bless you in the land He is giving you"* (Deuteronomy 28:8, NIV) would come to mind. I thought that was strange, but nevertheless, we continued to move forward.

GOD HAS GOOD PLANS FOR EACH ONE OF US, BUT WE MUST BE WILLING TO TAKE THE STEPS NECESSARY TO MAKE IT HAPPEN.

Believing that we had a chance to get it, I went ahead and began to add a few new employees. The down payment was ready and preliminary negotiations had begun, but a week later I read in the paper that the company that was selling the centers had chosen to do business with someone else. When they called to tell me the news, I felt an immediate disappointment but a certain peace at the same time.

Interestingly enough, at church the following Sunday, Pastor Pearson spoke about not always looking at the seen, but accepting and believing in the unseen. He said that just because something seemed evident didn't necessarily make it a reality and that there was much more for us (unseen) than against us (seen).

But the fact of the matter was that we had been outbid, so we let it go. When I prayed about the whole issue, God kept reminding me of what I had been reading and saying as part of the "Penix Family Blessings": *"The LORD your God will bless you in the land He is giving you."*

"That is crazy," I thought to myself. "Nobody is giving anyone anything in this deal." Then I specifically felt I should remove the contract that I had submitted, even though they had told me they were doing business with someone else. I immediately called and canceled my contract. My business mind knew that when a contract is outbid and you are told that the deal is over, your contract is automatically cancelled, but I knew when I was being led to do something contrary to what my business mind said.

With that done, Laurie and I refocused on our work with the other centers. A week later, the same person called from the company to say that the other deal fell apart. "Now we want to do business with you," he said. "You have a good reputation and we believe you can make this work. We'll accept your contract."

I immediately said, "What contract? I pulled it last week."

He replied, "I understand, just initial the old contract and we'll accept it."

Then I said, "I really don't want to offer that same contract because I don't want to pay as much as I did then. We are out some money, having hired new people, preparation, etc."

He said, "Well, how much do you want to pay for it?"

Half-joking, I said, "I don't want to pay anything for it."

After a long pause, he said, "O.K., make the contract for a one dollar so that it is legal. It's costing us so much a month just to operate the buildings and we need out of the deal."

Here he was, offering me both buildings, with contents and renovations valued at over $3 million, for only one dollar! God had said He wanted to bless me in the land that He was giving me. Well, I could certainly handle the dollar part.

Before he hung up, he joked, "Make sure you bring your dollar."

When Laurie and I took inventory in the 47,000 sq. ft area after we closed on the deal, the only money we found was a one dollar bill taped to a piece of cardboard. It was then that I remembered what God had said, "I will bless you in the land I *gave* you." God is very exact in His Word. We could not spend a dollar on something God said He would give us!

BLESSED COMING IN AND BLESSED GOING OUT

We had children from other centers on waiting lists that would want to go to our new centers. Also, we knew some of the children who were currently enrolled would stay. All in all, we were confident that we could fill both buildings in short order. Everything was falling into place like clockwork! We immediately started preparing both childcare centers to do business, as we were accustomed.

In the midst of everything, Billy Joe Daugherty, pastor of the Victory Christian Center church that was just down the street, came over to visit and asked, "We need extra space for our children's ministry. It's overflowing. Would you consider renting one of these buildings to us?"

I explained that due to liability issues, I would rather not let anyone rent the facilities. He thanked me and left, only to return a few weeks later with, "Would you consider selling both buildings to us?"

I replied, "Absolutely not!"

We had worked for two months, twelve to fourteen hours a day, cleaning, organizing, and sorting what was in both childcare centers. We were simultaneously enrolling children, doing a marketing blitz in the area, sharing the vision with every parent we met, and hiring new employees. We were in full swing and our business was on a role. We were about to break even with all the expenses and double our size with these two new centers, and now some pastor wants to buy the whole thing out from under us? Not a chance!

I told him about the one dollar miracle and how God had brought this whole project together. As we talked, however, something happened in my heart. I didn't know it at the time, but my destiny was being redefined.

Laurie and I talked about it, prayed about it, and talked about it some more. This was, interestingly enough, the same church we had seeded money into years earlier to help its child-care center grow and expand. I didn't know why I was doing it, but I felt in my heart that we should let them buy the entire inventory and renovations from us and assume our lease on the buildings, and Laurie agreed!

When the deal was all said and done, Victory Christian Center took over the leases that we had negotiated and the two buildings for just over $600,000. Had they obtained the 47,000 square feet full of new equipment and supplies any other way, it would have cost them over $3 million! It was an unexpected blessing, both for them and for us. We were blessed coming in and blessed going out—just as we were speaking over ourselves as part of the "Penix Family Blessings."

We were able to finish our dream home now, but my business mind kept telling me, "You left over $2.5 million on the table!" I could probably have sold the building, contents and business for more than $3 million had I taken the time to sell to someone else. I even told Pastor Billy Joe, "If God tells you to give us more money on this deal, don't feel like you have to pass it by me first, just obey." His response was, "Henry, I would rather pray that God blesses you and your remaining businesses." I was thinking in the back of my mind, "That was an easy way out," but I didn't say anything. Laurie and I were in agreement and we considered the money we "left on the table" to be seed into Billy Joe's ministry. Now the deal was done and we were back to six Koala Care centers and a somewhat regular life.

To our surprise, about three months later, we were in contact with the same company that had bid against us for the two childcare centers we had just sold to Victory. They wanted to know if we would ever consider selling our remaining six centers!

What an absurd idea! We were planning to go national. Why would we want to sell out now? This could never be of God—or could it?

PRINCIPLES FOR ACCELERATION

1. Aim to accelerate.

Believing that acceleration is possible is one of the first steps toward accelerating your destiny.

2. Give God the credit.

Though you are the one who needs to walk it out step by step, God is the one who is directing your steps, making the impossible possible. Always give Him the credit.

3. Implant the Word into your life.

If you don't know what you are capable of becoming, how will you reach your full potential? God's Word will unlock more than you could even imagine!

4. Listen to the Holy Spirit.

The Holy Spirit leads and guides you in all things, so it only makes sense that you go along with what He says. Pay attention to that small still voice inside of you. He sees the big picture, so trust Him.

5. Remain open to change.

When you refuse to change, you begin to slow down and even slide backward. Those who are willing to change are the ones who lead the way.

6. Keep your good name.

A good name is better than gold. No matter the prize, always guard your name—it is not replaceable.

80

7. Lean not on your own understanding.

No matter what your business mind says or what has been successful for you in the past, listen to what your spirit is saying. Since God is spirit, He can only speak to us through our spirit. That is why we are told to worship Him in spirit and in truth (John 4:24). Listen and you will hear.

Principles for Acceleration

CHAPTER EIGHT

ONE SEASON ENDS AND ANOTHER BEGINS

We had long-term vision for our business and our future. We were excited, we were in our destiny, and we were both in agreement. Everything was lined up and in working order. It just didn't make sense that we should sell our six remaining centers to one of the top childcare chains in the industry, with over 600 locations across the nation.

Our immediate response was, "No possible way!" but the more we thought about it, we had to honestly ask ourselves, "What if this really is God's plan for our life?"

We had always said we would pray and walk into opportunities, believing that if something wasn't of God that He would close the doors. The walking was always toward things we liked— a new home, a new center, a new opportunity—this was toward something we had never before considered. *Did we have the faith to walk toward the possibility of selling the business and let Him direct the outcome?*

We prayed about it and cautiously walked toward it...and the doors stayed open. Since we were being asked to do what we hadn't ever really thought about doing before, we figured we might as well be outrageous and ask for exactly what we wanted. Why not? They were the ones wanting what we had spent years perfecting! Unbelievably, they ultimately agreed to just about everything we asked for, so we kept watching and praying and walking.

They flew their CFO and Accountant down and asked how we implemented and maintained the budgets. They liked our computer program that tracked the money per center, gave cumulative totals at the push of a button, and kept everyone on track. They asked, "How could we implement something like this into our existing centers?"

Oddly enough, they represented the very company that had fired Laurie when she had worked for them several years earlier for trying to implement her new ideas. During negotiations when we told them about this, they laughed and said, "It would have been a whole lot cheaper had we just listened to her advice back then!"

Discussions continued for about three months, at which point they paid us several million dollars to wipe out all the debt we owed on all land and on every building we had purchased and built up until that point. We had officially sold our operating company! They took over insurance, payroll, and operations as they were. We didn't know it at the time, but our centers were one of the only centers, that after purchasing, they left as they were. Other than internal means of reporting to their corporate headquarters, they didn't change a thing about our program because they didn't need to! We saw that as a testimony of God's wisdom and creativity through us.

When the deal was complete, we were even able to retain ownership of all our buildings and land—debt free! The purchasing company signed a long-term lease agreement with us for our buildings, with long-term options! All told, the deal was worth over $20 million! All of a sudden we were the lenders and not the borrowers—something else we had spoken in the "Penix Family Blessings."

FROM LAURIE'S PERSPECTIVE
GIVING UP YOUR VISION

I had just written a full-scale accreditation program when the national childcare chain offered to buy us out. Why would I want to do all that work and then lose it? At the same time, I saw the call on Henry's life becoming more and more evident. He had supported me in Koala Care, which was really my dream and my vision. He stepped in and helped make it come to pass. Now things were changing and I saw him being directed by God like never before. What was I going to do, pursue my dream or pursue God's dream for us?

I began to really feel like it was Henry's time. I also felt a strong pull to be with my children (then ages thirteen, ten, and eight). They needed me like never before. They were not used to me being at home and taking care of them, cooking, etc. Everyone would go through a change. Was I willing to change and refocus my vision? Yes.

A NEW DESTINY

A few months later, the company that bought us out stopped buying additional childcare centers and dissolved their acquisitions department. And on top of it, they were probably the only company that we would have ever sold to. The timing was perfect. Had we missed that window of opportunity, our destiny would have been delayed.

Getting out of the childcare business went against everything we had ever done or planned for, but here we were in an entirely different position. What would we do now that we didn't need to manage 300 employees, 1500+ children, and work what seemed like twenty-four hours a day? God obviously had a vision for our future.

EVERY DESTINY IS A SEASON.

For some time, opportunities had been coming for me to speak with other individuals and groups about what we had been through and about how they could find their destiny by following the same principles we had. It seemed simple—finding and walking in the destiny that God had designed—yet the results were incredibly powerful!

I loved seeing people's eyes light up with hope and expectation for their own future, but I had to ask myself, "Is this what God wants me to do full-time?" Speaking to others about God's principles and His Word would make me what I had vowed I would never become: a minister!

Laurie didn't want to be married to a minister either! What I didn't realize at the time was that she was taking this transition much more seriously than I imagined. She was comfortable with childcare and could handle all the related responsibilities, but this "ministry thing" was more than she could handle. She didn't tell me, but a lump had appeared under her skin and would not go away. She began to get sicker and sicker by the day. She ended up talking with doctors who examined her and tried to diagnose her illness. As for the lump, they were dumbfounded.

"I thought I was going to die," Laurie explains, "Not because I was sick, but because I felt my purpose in life was over." It was a mental and spiritual battle that was raging inside of her. When she prayed and knew that she had purpose, the lump was gone within twenty-four hours! So much for those "Holy Rollers" she all but mocked just a few years earlier!

Looking back, Laurie says, "I thought we were going the wrong way. When I realized the devil was trying to get me to stop walking towards our destiny, I knew exactly what to do: put my faith in God and support my husband. The lump and illness never returned."

I had my own challenges to deal with. I was having panic attacks about getting up and speaking in front of people. I had never had trouble before, but when I realized that this was my new destiny, the pressure increased dramatically. I would be about to speak and an almost uncontrollable urge would come over me to leave the room or auditorium where I was speaking. I was anxious and nervous like never before. This was something much greater than just "stage fright."

When I realized that this was not my normal self, I understood that it was a spiritual attack against my destiny. After prayer and taking bold steps to do what God was calling me to do, the panic attacks disappeared. God continued to minister to me saying, "Perfect love will get rid of all fear." When I speak now, my love for the people and desire to see their lives bettered by something I may have to say causes all fear to disappear. I have not had a panic attack since.

In both of our cases, the devil was trying to throw up a smoke screen to divert our attention away from what we knew to be our destiny. If he could destroy our vision in its infancy, when any vision is most vulnerable to attack, we would never reach our destiny. We knew however, that God had a good plan for our lives and we were committed to walking it out.

STEPPING INTO YOUR DESTINY

Why do people hesitate about walking into the unknown? I think it is because they are afraid. Letting go of fear will always require grabbing hold of faith, and that is where many people stop. They don't want to let go of the comfortable, the experienced, or the normal. It takes faith to go where you have never gone before and to believe in a dream you've never seen before.

Faith is a necessary part of life. When we came to terms with this reality, it made much more sense that God would require us to walk by faith. If we already had everything we needed to obtain our vision, we wouldn't need God. But we need faith to please God, for *"without faith it is impossible to please God"*

(Hebrews 11:6, NIV). Everyone, in some way, shape, or form, will need faith to walk out his or her own destiny.

There are practical steps to take as you walk into your destiny. By first writing down on paper what it is you feel you should do, you will then have a better understanding of what the first step might be. Then simply take the first step. When Laurie and I weren't sure what that first step was, we always found someone successfully doing what we want to do and learned from them. Before long, progress was noticeable. As we kept taking steps forward, our destiny became clear.

INSANITY IS DOING THE SAME THING OVER AND OVER AGAIN, YET EXPECTING DIFFERENT RESULTS. SOMETIMES YOU NEED TO TAKE A DIFFERENT ROUTE TO GET WHERE YOU WANT TO GO.

As far as our destiny with our childcare centers, that destiny was passing. We redirected our focus out of obedience to God, realizing that our time in the childcare business was for a reason and for a season. Yes, He blessed us and we were successful at it, but for a reason: God was preparing us to accelerate into our true destiny.

Everyone will arrive at a destination at some point in his or her life, but is that destination your true destiny? Never be discouraged and think that everything up until this point in your life has been a waste. Romans 8:28 says, *"And we know that all things work together for good to them that love God, to them who are the called according to his purpose"* (KJV). Just as in our life, God used our past to prepare us and help us in our future. Everything I learned at the Fortune 150 Corporation I used in childcare. Everything I learned in growing a childcare business, I am now able to use in the ministry. Life cycles and everything counts. If you submit your life to God and go where He directs, you will reach your destiny. Without God, you cannot arrive at your destiny because every destiny is based on God's plan for your life.

If God has good things in store for you, and He does, then why wouldn't you want to walk in your destiny, receiving those good things? You don't have to understand everything first—you just need to accept the vision or desire He has given you and take the first step in that direction.

Interestingly enough, the word "desire" comes from the Latin word "sire," which means "of the father." In short, when you have accepted Christ, what you want in life or your desires are from your Father in heaven anyway. As you are in Him and His words are in you, ask whatever you desire and you will get it!

Your desire isn't there to cause chaos or confusion; it is there because God has given it to you. Rest in the fact that when God puts a desire in your heart, He also gives you everything you need to make that desire come true. Your job is to walk toward your destiny, one small step at a time and let Him direct your footsteps. Be faithful over the few things that God has placed in your hands now, and He will make you ruler over many, just like He did for Laurie and me in every area of our life.

PRINCIPLES FOR ACCELERATION

1. Know the season.

There will come a time when the season you are in will change. Be willing to let your desires and visions change as well.

2. Don't be afraid of money.

*Money will not make you proud or unholy; neither will the lack of money. Money is simply a tool **to be used wisely**. Many great things can be accomplished with money. If you're faithful over few (even the money you have now), God will give you many.*

3. Be willing to do what you vowed you'd never do.

Life is strange in that you often end up doing what you say you will never do. Remain open to the impossible—because it will probably happen.

4. Recognize when you are in a battle.

As a Christian, you will be under spiritual attack, sometimes worse than others. Recognize this and be ready to stand your ground and trust in God.

5. Arrive at your destiny, not just any destination.

Everyone will end up at a destination in life, but not everyone will end up at his or her destiny. Your destiny is for you to fulfill—now walk towards it.

6. Step out in faith.

Life doesn't come on a silver platter. To reach your dreams, it will require that you step out in faith—God will respond!

7. Accept the desires in your heart.

If you are in Christ and His words are in you, the desires you have are from God. Accept them, no matter how "unbelievable" or big they might seem, and then pursue them with everything you have.

8. If you can't stay on track, your vision is too small.

If anything diverts your attention from walking towards your vision, then your vision is probably too small. To get something you've never gotten, you must do something you've never done. Pursue your vision with passion!

"PENIX FAMILY BLESSINGS"

God's Word says that I am the head and not the tail, I am first and not last, I am above and not beneath. God commands me to be blessed in anything I do. God wishes above all things that I prosper and be in health, even as my soul prospers. I am blessed in the city, blessed at my job, and blessed in my school.

My children are blessed, my spouse is blessed, and my mom and dad are blessed. My businesses are blessed and my bank accounts are blessed. I am blessed when I come in and I am blessed when I go out. *God will bless me in the land He gave me.* God gave me the power to get wealth, homes, cars, businesses, toys, vacations, boats, motorcycles, land, and anything else I want. I will lend and not borrow.

Jesus said if I have the faith of a grain of mustard seed and say to the mountain be removed and cast into the sea and believe in my heart, it shall be done. I see debt as a mountain in my life and I command it to be removed and never come back. I will be financially blessed to bless other people who are in need and to help spread the Word of God throughout the world. I will never be afraid of anything and I can do all things through Christ who makes me strong. Goodness and mercy shall follow me all the days of my long healthy life. God is perfecting everything that I am concerned about.

By Jesus' stripes I am healed. Sickness cannot live in my body. If sickness or disease tries to enter my body, it will have to die when it touches my body, because by Jesus' stripes I am healed. The Lord is my light to show me where to go and my salvation to save me from any harm. God has put angels in charge to protect me. Angels will always protect me from any harm and I will not fear anything. Jesus gives me strength and makes me strong. If anyone comes against me or tries to harm me, they will stumble and fall.

I will always follow God and keep His commandments. I will have a long healthy life, a healthy trim body, a close loving family, and wealth and prosperity in all areas of my life. I am blessed and I will be successful in anything I do. I love Jesus and Jesus loves me. Angels, I command you to always protect me. I will receive all the blessings of God because God said I would. If I need or desire anything, I will use my co-creative power given to me by God to speak my need or desire into existence and believe that I have received it, never doubting, until what I have spoken comes to me. After I receive what I have spoken, I will give thanks and praise unto God. When people ask how I can receive the desires of my heart, I will tell them that God gives them to me and I will thank God for all His blessings in my life.

Today will be a great day and I will prosper in everything I do. I am in perfect health and nothing will harm me. I will walk in the favor and anointing of God and everything I do will prosper.

We would say this as a family nearly everyday. If we couldn't meet together in the morning, the kids would say it on the way to school. We did not repeat this out of unbelief, we were training our minds to think differently and to expect the impossible!

Life Stress Test

Directions: Put an "x" beside every stressful event that applies to you.

___Death of Spouse—*100 points*
___Change in work responsibilities—*29 points*
___Divorce—*73 points*
___Trouble with in-laws—*29 points*
___Marital Separation—*65 points*
___Outstanding personal achievement—*28 points*
___Jail Term—*63 points*
___Spouse begins or stops work—*26 points*
___Death of close family member—*63 points*
___Starting or finishing school—*26 points*
___Personal injury or illness—*53 points*
___Change in living conditions—*25 points*
___Marriage—*50 points*
___Revision of personal habits—*24 points*
___Fired from work—*47 points*
___Trouble with boss—*23 points*
___Marital reconciliation—*45 points*
___Change in work hours, conditions—*20 points*
___Retirement—*45 points*
___Change in residence—*20 points*
___Change in family member's health—*44 points*
___Change in schools—*20 points*
___Pregnancy—*40 points*
___Change in recreational habits—*19 points*
___Sex difficulties—*39 points*

___Change in church activities—*19 points*

___Addition to family—*39 points*

___Change in social activities—*18 points*

___Business readjustment—*39 points*

___Mortgage or loan under $10,000—*17 points*

___Change in financial status—*38 points*

___Change in sleeping habits—*16 points*

___Death of close friend—*37 points*

___Change in number of family gatherings—*15 points*

___Change to a different line of work—*36 points*

___Change in eating habits—*15 points*

___Change in number of marital arguments—*35 points*

___Vacation—*13 points*

___Mortgage or loan over $10,000—*31 points*

___Christmas season—*12 points*

___Foreclosure of mortgage or loan—*30 points*

___Minor violations of the law—*11 points*

Add the points that correspond to items you place an "x" beside.

<u>**Your grand total**</u>: _____

<u>**Scores:**</u>

> 0-149 points—you have a low susceptibility to stress-related illness
>
> 150-299 points—you have a medium susceptibility to stress-related illness
>
> 300+ points—you have a high susceptibility to stress-related illness—if you scored 300 or above, make sure you read this book thoroughly!

PRINCIPLES FOR ACCELERATION

CHAPTER 2
PRINCIPLES FOR ACCELERATION

1. Prepare and begin with the end in mind.

Before you build a building, why wouldn't you calculate the costs in advance? It would be pretty embarrassing to be half finished and run out of money.

2. "See" things as they will be.

It takes belief in yourself and in what you are doing to "see" what others cannot. Put action to your words and you will be on your way!

3. Be willing to step out into the unknown.

Every great accomplishment began as a great risk. A hero is always defined by the size of his opponent—the greater the opponent, the greater the hero. Those who take the risks are the ones who reap the rewards.

4. Be faithful with the little that you have.

If you can successfully and faithfully manage little, the day will inevitably come when you can and will successfully manage a lot.

5. Don't spend what you do not have.

Debt has a way of choking the life out of your business, your marriage, and your future. If you don't have it, don't spend it—then you won't owe it!

6. Keep your word no matter what!

Those who keep their word are destined for success, while those who refuse to keep their word are destined for failure—this is true in business and in life!

7. Communicate honestly with everyone you do business with.

Communicate with everyone the same way you would like to be communicated with. You can't go wrong!

8. Don't limit your dreams to what you currently see.

Keep the window of opportunity open—you might be surprised to find that the vision that seems so big to you now is actually part of something even bigger

CHAPTER 3
PRINCIPLES FOR ACCELERATION

1. Don't chase money.

Money is necessary, useful, and good to have, but you cannot buy love, peace, happiness, joy, friends, or a good marriage with it. Money is NOT the root of all evil; the love of money is. Put your priorities in order with God first and there is a way to have it all!

2. Stick with your priorities.

You will always do what you want to do—so keep your priorities in proper order and in front of you at all times. Stay focused!

3. Make your marriage unbreakable.

Decide that nothing will come between you and your spouse. Then live each day with that reality in mind. A house divided against itself cannot stand.

4. Make decisions together.

Those who work together must make decisions together. It is one of the best ways to bond (or break) a working relationship. Don't allow your relationship to be played from the middle by other people. Communicate!

5. Resolve arguments quickly.

Instead of letting the chasm widen, make it a point to resolve an argument as quickly as possible. Don't go to bed mad—you will sleep much better!

99

6. Learn to really listen to your spouse.

> *Learn to listen as you would like to be listened to. You might discover something you never knew before—about yourself!*

7. Don't rush God.

> *If you "give" a difficult issue to God, let Him work it out His way. Don't rush Him! He is the best at what He does. You are the only one who can get in your way!*

CHAPTER 4
PRINCIPLES FOR ACCELERATION

1. Sell the vision.

Sell your vision until the right people buy it who can help you achieve it. At that point, your job will be much easier. People die without a vision; mentally, emotionally, and sometimes physically.

2. Knowledge without wisdom is useless.

You have to mix the two together. When we take what we learn and add that to God's wisdom that He gives us, we can expect the extraordinary!

3. Take the first step toward multiplication.

Taking the first step is the hardest part of multiplication and increase, but once you get the ball rolling, it builds momentum and gets easier by the day.

4. See it, then take action.

Walk toward your dreams. It is not enough to have the dream, you must take the necessary practical steps toward making it into a reality, day by day.

5. Set goals as you need them.

Along the way, set specific short-term goals and personal rewards for achieving those goals. This will motivate, encourage, and keep you going. It will also add more fuel to your fire—making you burn longer with stronger passion.

6. Step out of your comfort zone.

Don't be afraid to step out of your comfort zone—the place that you feel secure or comfortable. Do it today. Tomorrow you will say, "I wish I had done it earlier." To get what you've never had, you must do what you've never done.

7. Pursue peace.

You cannot buy peace. When you have peace in your heart that you are where you need to be and doing the right thing, don't trade that peace for anything, not even money!

CHAPTER 5
PRINCIPLES FOR ACCELERATION

1. Say "no" to fear.

Fear is nothing more than False Evidence Appearing Real (F.E.A.R.). Don't listen to it! You can only hold on to faith or fear, not both.

2. Take care of your people.

The more you show your appreciation for your employees, the better they will perform, and the more you show your appreciation for them, the better they will perform, and the more you...

3. Play it safe and do what it takes.

Most businesses fail within the first two years due to financial problems. Being conservative now will more than pay for itself in the end!

4. Don't be afraid to walk away.

Not every great opportunity is as great as it might appear. For whatever the reason, if you don't have peace about something, don't do it. Success is never in a hurry, but we are.

5. Dream BIG.

You will spend the same amount of time in any given day working on your dream, big or small. Choose BIG.

6. Believe you CAN do it.

Begin with the premise that you CAN do it and then focus on your goal. Don't listen to the "advice" (discouraging words) of your friends—your faith is not in them anyway.

7. Don't take "no" for an answer.

If you are pursuing your dreams and you know God has opened the door, then keep going. The answer you seek will eventually come.

8. Get in motion.

It is much easier to move an object in motion than it is to move a stationary object. The same law of physics applies to you and the Holy Spirit; He leads, but nothing can be led unless it is first in motion.

CHAPTER 6
PRINCIPLES FOR ACCELERATION

1. Make setbacks your green light.

When setbacks slow you down, resist the urge to quit or even look down. See setbacks as a green light to press forward with increased effort.

2. Return spite with kindness.

Give the people who act spitefully toward you the benefit of the doubt and treat them with kindness. They may become your greatest allies!

3. Give out of obedience.

If you feel you should give someone (even a competitor) your time, talent, or money, then do it. Obedience to God is your ticket to accelerating your destiny.

4. See personal growth as vital.

Personal growth is the foundation for all long-term business success. It is the base on which everything else is built!

5. Make time for your family.

You will not find the time for family; you must **make** *the time. When you do, your schedule has an amazing ability to work itself around your priorities.*

6. Blow through smoke screens.

When it comes to your destiny, smoke screens are inevitable. Maintain your course and you'll blow through every one of them. Never mistake a smoke screen for a closed door; keep moving forward.

7. Walk by faith and not by sight.

Even if things don't "appear" to be going the way you thought, know that a good idea may come to pass, but a God idea **must** *come to pass!*

CHAPTER 7
PRINCIPLES FOR ACCELERATION

1. Aim to accelerate.

Believing that acceleration is possible is one of the first steps toward accelerating your destiny.

2. Give God the credit.

Though you are the one who needs to walk it out step by step, God is the one who is directing your steps, making the impossible possible. Always give Him the credit.

3. Implant the Word into your life.

If you don't know what you are capable of becoming, how will you reach your full potential? God's Word will unlock more than you could even imagine!

4. Listen to the Holy Spirit.

The Holy Spirit leads and guides you in all things, so it only makes sense that you go along with what He says. Pay attention to that small still voice inside of you. He sees the big picture, so trust Him.

5. Remain open to change.

When you refuse to change, you begin to slow down and even slide backward. Those who are willing to change are the ones who lead the way.

6. Keep your good name.

A good name is better than gold. No matter the prize, always guard your name—it is not replaceable.

7. Lean not on your own understanding.

No matter what your business mind says or what has been successful for you in the past, listen to what your spirit is saying. Since God is spirit, He can only speak to us through our spirit. That is why we are told to worship Him in spirit and in truth (John 4:24, KJV). Listen and you will hear.

CHAPTER 8
PRINCIPLES FOR ACCELERATION

1. Know the season.

There will come a time when the season you are in will change. Be willing to let your desires and visions change as well.

2. Don't be afraid of money.

Money will not make you proud or unholy; neither will the lack of money. Money is simply a tool to be used wisely. Many great things can be accomplished with money. If you're faithful over few (even the money you have now), God will give you many.

3. Be willing to do what you vowed you'd never do.

Life is strange in that you often end up doing what you say you will never do. Remain open to the impossible— because it will probably happen.

4. Recognize when you are in a battle.

As a Christian, you will be under spiritual attack, some- times worse than others. Recognize this and be ready to stand your ground and trust in God.

5. Arrive at your destiny, not just any destination.

Everyone will end up at a destination in life, but not every- one will end up at his or her destiny. Your destiny is for you to fulfill—now walk towards it.

6. Step out in faith.

Life doesn't come on a silver platter. To reach your dreams, it will require that you step out in faith—God will respond!

7. Accept the desires in your heart.

If you are in Christ and His words are in you, the desires you have are from God. Accept them, no matter how "unbelievable" or big they might seem, and then pursue them with everything you have.

8. If you can't stay on track, your vision is too small.

If anything diverts your attention from walking towards your vision, then your vision is probably too small. To get something you've never gotten, you must do something you've never done. Pursue your vision with passion!

WORKBOOK

FIVE KEYS TO
ACCELERATE
YOUR DESTINY

Table of Contents

* Please note, this is the same type of workbook I used when setting my goals. Try to complete this in one sitting and most importantly, when you are finished, take that first action step! There is power in momentum! This is not about something that <u>might</u> work—What I am sharing with you is something that <u>did</u> work, and this can work for you as well!

INTRODUCTION

Congratulations! By reading this book and beginning this workbook, you have just taken that significant first step toward accelerating your destiny! You have separated yourself from the other 97 percent of the population who won't take that first step. You are now in the top 3 percent. An interesting study was done on a graduating class at Yale University. They asked who had written down their goals in life and only 3 percent responded. Upon following this 3 percent who actually wrote down their goals for twenty years, they found that those 3 percent made more money than the other 97 percent combined! I know this isn't all about money, but whatever you're striving for, know that the first step is to write your vision down.

Remember to pray that the Holy Spirit, who leads, guides, and teaches us in all things, will give you wisdom, clarity, and direction as you complete this workbook. These principals will work for anyone. However, they worked in my life with such speed and clarity because of my personal relationship with Jesus Christ. If you haven't made a decision to acknowledge Jesus as your Lord, please go to the special offer (Section V) of this workbook before you get started. It will help tremendously.

Now let's begin with some basic understandings of our desires and how they relate to our destiny:

#1. The desires you have in your heart are not there by accident.

The word "desire" comes from the Latin root word "sire," which means "of the father." So when you get a desire in your heart, know that your Creator has placed it there, your Father, God in heaven. He didn't just give it to you to cause confusion or make you wish for something you could never obtain. What's more, Scripture says that God wants to give you the desires of your heart.

#2. God is no respecter of persons, but He is a respecter of faith.

When you put faith demands on God, He will answer. You can actually start living like what you have desired is real, you call what isn't as though it already is and then walk and believe in it until it comes to pass. Dare to expect the unbelievable from God; He will not let you down, but remember to always give him the glory.

#3. You already have what you need to make your desires come true.

God has given you the faith, the power, the anointing, and the ability to make your desires come true. As you are in Christ, the power is in YOU!

You have certain desires that God has placed in your heart. He has given you the power to make those desires a reality and He has already ordered your footsteps. If you stub your toe as you walk toward your destiny, He has promised that goodness and mercy will follow you all the days of your life. God has got your back covered, He has ordered your footsteps, and He desires that you prosper in all that you do, confirming His covenant with you. Now the bottom line is this: **it is now up to you to believe in your heart that you will obtain the desires of your heart and take the necessary steps to get you there.** You are the only one who can get in your way! You are also the only one who can walk in your destiny, obtaining the desires of your heart!

Here are the FIVE keys God gave me that I implemented into my life that brought forth the desires of my heart. These keys empowered me to walk in and accelerate my destiny:

Key #1

Discover your vision—
What is the desire of your heart?

Several years ago the world-famous golfer, Arnold Palmer, was asked to play golf with the king of Saudi Arabia. Arnold accepted and was quickly whisked to Saudi Arabia in a private jet. They played golf for a few days and had a great time together. As Arnold was getting ready to leave, the king said, "I want to give you something. It is customary that when I invite guests here I also give them something as a token of our meeting."

Arnold graciously declined, saying, "I don't need anything. Just playing golf here was more than enough!"

But the king insisted until Arnold said, "O.K., I collect golf clubs, so if you must give me something, I would accept a golf club."

The king said, "Alright, I will give you a golf club."

On the jet heading home, Arnold found himself thinking, "What kind of a golf club would a king give me? Is it going to

IF YOU HAVE ALL THE MONEY IN THE WORLD AND YOU DON'T HAVE GOOD FAMILY RELATIONSHIPS, HEALTH, JOY, OR PEACE OF MIND, THE MONEY IS NOT WORTH ANYTHING.

have diamonds on it? Is it going to be gold? What's it going to be like?"

A few days later there was a knock on Arnold's door and a courier delivered an envelope. Inside was the title deed to a golf club—an entire GOLF CLUB! Not the type you swing but the type of club where you go to play golf!

Such is the mindset of a king! Admittedly, it is a little different than the way most of us think. Now consider the fact that our Father in heaven is not just a king, but the *King of Kings*. His mindset for us, for our vision, and for our destiny, far exceeds anything we could ever ask or imagine. If you realize that **your father** is the King of Kings, what would you ask for?

YOUR VISION AND DESTINY

Scripture says that *"we are God's workmanship, created in Christ Jesus to do good works, which God prepared in advance for us to do"* (Ephesians 2:10, NIV). This means that God has pre-finished good works for us to do. It is up to us to walk in the destiny He already ordained for us. We aren't forced to—we get to!

I believe the decisions we make from today onwards will determine if we will walk in the good things we were predestined to walk in or not. God has an incredible destiny in store for us. Our job is to accept that and to move into it.

To fully reach our destiny, we need a vision for our future. Scripture says that without a vision, people will perish. What is your vision? What is it that God has put in your heart—maybe that idea or little thing you have always wanted to do? And please don't let money be an obstacle. Everything I ever did started with not enough money.

Think of it this way. If I were to place 1 billion dollars in your bank account today that grew at a reasonable 10 percent each year, *you would have to spend $270,000 every day, 365 days* *a year, for the rest of your life just to avoid making more money from the interest you would be earning!* Every morning you woke up you would have to think about how you would spend $270,000 because the next day you would have to do it all over again. Your children and grandchildren would continue when you died because the money would never run out!

With that mindset, what would your vision be now? Would that thing God has placed in your heart be a little bit bigger? The desire in your heart is your vision, but before you actually write your vision down, consider the following:

◈ Your father is the King of Kings!
◈ You're an heir to the kingdom of God!
◈ Your brother is Jesus!
◈ You can do all things through Christ who strengthens you!
◈ There is NO LIMIT to what God can do!

So now what is that desire in your heart? What would you want to do if there were no limitations...*because there are no limitations!* The only limitations are the ones we create in our minds.

ACTION STEPS TO GET YOU THERE

WRITE DOWN YOUR VISION

Habakkuk 2:2-3 says, *"And the LORD answered me, and said, 'Write the vision, and make it plain upon tables, that he may run that readeth it. For the vision is yet for an appointed time, but at the end it shall speak, and not lie: though it tarry, wait for it; because it will surely come, it will not tarry'"* (KJV).

The vision my wife and I had many years ago that we wrote down and then took the steps to walk in and work towards **is taking place right now!** Our vision is for this appointed time and is speaking to you, encouraging you to take that first step.

Now take the first step and **write your vision down.** My vision is:

_____

_____

_____

_____

_____

_____

KEY #2

TAKE THE FIRST STEPS TO PUT YOUR VISION INTO ACTION

Once we write down our vision, we have to honestly ask ourselves, "What am I going to do to implement it? What steps are we taking every day to walk toward our vision?"

Many people have great ideas and then sit around and expect God to drop the finished product in their lap. God won't do that. He says:

"I give **you** the power to get wealth to confirm my covenant" (*"But thou shalt remember the LORD thy God: for it is he that giveth thee power to get wealth, that he may establish his covenant which he swore unto thy fathers, as it is this day"* Deuteronomy 8:18, KJV).

"I will prosper the work of **your** hands" (*"The LORD thy God shall bless thee in all thine increase, and in all the **works of thine hands**"* Deuteronomy 16:15, KJV).

Clearly, God wants to work **through you** and **your hands**, not against you.

You have probably heard the Chinese proverb: the journey of a thousand miles always begins with the first step. Though obviously true, if you look at your vision as being a huge thousand-mile journey and you have to walk to get there, you probably won't even get up and start walking because you are thinking, "There is no possible way I can walk a thousand miles!"

Thankfully, the wisdom and guiding of the Holy Spirit is there to help you take the first small step. When Jesus ascended to heaven, He said, "I'll send the Holy Spirit who will lead, guide, and teach you in all things" [*"Nevertheless I tell you the truth; It is expedient for you that I go away: for if I go not away, the Comforter will not come unto you; but if I depart, I will send him unto you* (John 16:7, KJV), and *"Howbeit when he, the Spirit of truth, is come, he will guide you into all truth: for he shall not speak of himself; but whatsoever he shall hear, that shall he speak: and he will show you things to come* (John 16:13, KJV)]. When you receive Christ, you have his Holy Spirit in you to direct your steps.

Then once you have taken the first step, He will lead your second step. You can not be led unless you are in motion! Every so often I take my children horseback riding. After they saddle their horses, I can just imagine one horse deciding to lie down in the grass. You obviously can't lead a horse that's lying down, much less ride it, but when it stands up and takes the first step, then and only then can it be led.

WHEN YOU DO WHAT YOU CAN, GOD WILL DO WHAT YOU CAN'T.

The same principle applies to walking out your vision. You take the first step—even if you're unsure of exactly where to step —and as you submit to the Holy Spirit He will continue to lead you. Once you are in motion, *you will be led*.

It probably won't happen overnight, but if you are faithful over the little that God puts in your hands now, He will give you more. The fact that my wife and I sold one of our businesses for $20 million dollars is a blessing today, but had that happened to me fifteen years ago, I would have self-destructed! But God, step by step, line upon line and precept upon precept, took me to the position where I could receive what He had for me. I didn't take all the right steps, but I was at least in motion and submissive to Him so that He could lead me.

You might be thinking, "O.K., I'm willing to take the first step toward my vision, *but what if I make a mistake?*" Good question—but God answered it when He promised you that *"goodness and mercy shall follow me all the days of my life"* (Psalms 23:6). If you make a mistake, goodness and mercy will be right behind you! God has set you up for success AND provided you a safety net. He has got your back! He will even cause all things to work out for your good, as Romans 8:28 states, *"And we know that all things work together for good to them that love God, to them who are the called according to his purpose"* (KJV).

In addition to being in motion, we must also be teachable. Not long ago my wife and I bought a VCR. We found one that could record up to three days in advance, filter out commercials, etc. It could do almost everything. So why is it then sometimes when I walk into people's homes, I see their VCR blinking "12:00...12:00...12:00"?

We all have the VCR's manual, but have we read it? And even if we have read it, have we taken the first step and walked over to the VCR to program it to be all the manufacturer said it could be? The blinking "12:00" is a dead giveaway.

God has given each of us our own instruction manual for life, the Bible, but have we read it? Even if we have read it, have we taken the first step to program ourselves to be all the manufacturer (our Creator) said we could be? Do we know the Word and believe it so we can say:

◆ To sickness and disease, *"by his stripes we are healed?"*
◆ To that mountain, *"be removed and cast into the sea."*
◆ To poverty and lack, *"let the poor say I am rich."*
◆ To weakness, *"let the weak say I am strong."*

You can say these things and get results because the manufacturer said you could. ***It's in the manual—the inspired Word of God***—but it is up to you to read the Word and program yourself for success in all areas of your life. God says, *"If you abide in Me, and My words abide in you, you will ask what you desire, and it shall be done for you"* (John 15:7, NKJV).

If you are in Him and His words are in you, you won't be asking for things out of His will for your life, like three purple elephants! Many people have gotten off on tangents here, thinking that they can name it and claim it, blab it and grab it, and it will all come to pass. That is not what God is saying. When you are in Him and have His Word in you, then you will be asking for what He desires for you—and it will come to pass. That is the best place to start toward implementing your vision.

ACTION STEPS TO GET YOU THERE

IMPLEMENT YOUR VISION

Right now, take the time to list ten things that you can do immediately to implement your vision. Your first step may be and probably should be prayer. Once you have written down the next nine things you could do that will ultimately move you towards your vision, give yourself a time-frame to compete the steps.

If you are unsure of what exactly to do, then just do research. Go out and find other people who have been successful doing what you want to do (or at least something similar). Be up front with people. Successful people love to talk about their successes. Become a sponge and absorb all you can, then combine what you learn with what God is showing you to do and you'll be on your way.

List at least ten things you can do right now along with a time-frame for their completion. Do the first one *today*—get in motion!

1._____   6._____

2._____   7._____

3._____   8._____

4._____   9._____

5._____   10._____

KEY #3

MONITOR YOUR PROGRESS—
SETTING BENCHMARKS

If you are measuring what you are doing, you are making progress. It's really that simple!

Years ago one of the first companies I worked for offered an all-expense-paid-trip to Hawaii if I made a certain number of sales within the year. I was excited about the challenge and wrote down my goals on a bar graph and posted it on my office wall. Everyday I would come in and color in the next level I reached after making sales.

There was a momentum building by the mere fact that I was monitoring my progress. Every time I left and walked out of that office, I was thinking subconsciously of returning and adding another sale to my graph. The whole sales staff noticed my graph, which meant I was now accountable to them! Now I had to do it.

By the end of the year, I was the only one in my branch office who had reached the goal, but everybody was supporting me because I was measuring it and they could see the progress. One of the main reasons that I reached my goal was because I constantly monitored my progress.

Part of successful monitoring also includes inspecting your progress. I could expect progress all day long, but until I *inspected* it, I had no way of enforcing it or knowing if I was progressing. When I was in the childcare business, I inspected the balance sheets and income statements every thirty days. I wanted to know

127

how my business had changed from last month to this month and how my business changed from last year to this year. How would I have known if I was growing unless I measured?

People are the same way. They will never do what you expect, but they will always do what you inspect. When we turn this principle on ourselves, we realize that we won't necessarily do things that aren't going to be inspected. In short, we need to be accountable to someone so that we are indeed going to do what we say we will do—and are moving towards our destiny. I always recommend being accountable to your spouse, but a trustworthy friend or associate will work as well.

Every morning, monitor your progress to see if you have at least taken a step toward your vision. It doesn't matter if you don't have the money, the time, the resources, or the connections. You are in the perfect spot to reach what you are aiming for because, Scripture says, *"But God has chosen the foolish things of the world to put to shame the wise, and God has chosen the weak things of the world to put to shame the things which are mighty"* (I Corinthians 1:27, KJV). People will call you foolish because you don't have what they think you need to succeed, but God **and** His Word are on your side. He will get glory by using you to confound the "wise" around you! You and God make a majority.

Just think, if you already had what it took to get what you needed, you wouldn't need God. Since it is impossible to please God without faith, and faith is doing something that you couldn't do on your own, then if you don't have the resources or connections necessary to obtain your vision, you are in a perfect position to exercise your faith, please God, and obtain your vision.

This is not a theory. This is His Word—and it works!

ACTION STEPS TO GET YOU THERE

MONITOR YOUR PROGRESS

What steps can you measure in moving towards your goal? List as many things as you can in the spaces below.

_____

_____

_____

_____

_____

Now, take some time to create your own chart, graph, or some other means by which you can monitor your progress. Whether you keep track of your efforts on your computer or on your wall, it makes no difference—just make sure you measure your progress on a daily basis and keep it where you will have to see it everyday. That is how you will know you are **making** progress toward your dreams and walking towards your destiny!

KEY #4

WHAT LEGACY WILL YOU LEAVE BEHIND?

So now that you have obtained and written your vision down, listed how you will implement it, and set up a plan to measure your progress—**what is it all for?** You will some day leave it all behind as your legacy. This means that everything you possess and everything you become will some day pass down to those who come after you.

What will you be leaving your spouse, your relatives, your neighbors, your co-workers, your friends, your city, your state, or your nation?

I take this very seriously today, but several years ago I was churning out nothing more than money-hungry attitudes, lack of peace, emptiness that drugs and alcohol couldn't fill, a bad relationship with my wife, and irresponsibility. I did have a black Porsche 911, but that wasn't worth a dime when I compared it to my overall legacy. I was trying to do things my way, leaving behind a meaningless legacy.

When you do it God's way, everything comes into balance, but is up to you to take the necessary steps to do it God's way. God wants you to possess the good land and to leave it as an inheritance for your children and your children's children (1 Chronicles 28:8). To do so will mean that we need to concentrate on more than just our bank accounts.

What passes down in a legacy? ***Absolutely everything!*** Love, joy, peace, and mannerisms, just to name a few. It can also be the habit of mom and dad throwing pots and pans at each other every time there is a fight. It could be the habit of running from bill collectors. It could even be rebellion, the thoughts you think, and actions you display when an authority figure tells you what to do.

Be introspective for a moment. Ask yourself, "Is what I am doing or who I have become really what I want to leave behind?" If it isn't, change it. If it is, keep at it. Either way, you now have the keys to bring your destiny to pass!

Action steps to get you there

Legacy worth leaving

Make a list of all the individuals who are in any way a recipient of your legacy. Put down every name that you can think of, then beside their names write what they will receive from your legacy.

List the legacies you will be able to leave once you've obtained the vision you wrote down at the beginning of this workbook (don't forget the intangibles).

Name   Legacy left behind

_____   _____

_____   _____

_____   _____

_____   _____

_____   _____

_____   _____

_____   _____

KEY #5

ACCEPT A
VERY SPECIAL OFFER

At the most basic level, Jesus gave up everything (His life included) so that you could have everything. He came to give, not to take. He wants you to experience life and find your destiny. To do so, you must recognize your need of His help. You can't do it on your own. How else do you explain the continual search for answers that have yet to be answered, even after thousands of years? Why am I here? Where am I going? Do I have a purpose in life?

You can have the answers to all of these questions, but even more important than that is the fact that God has an incredible destiny for you. To live it will require that you acknowledge Him as your Lord and Savior. He isn't a "do this, do that" kind of God, but He is 100 percent holy. This means that our sin (that we are born in and cannot help) and His perfection do not mix. Since He cannot change (why would He want to?), the only way we can connect with Him is for us to be washed clean or forgiven for our sins.

For many, myself included, I was ashamed of my past. I never thought I was good enough for God. I used to think the day that I stopped sinning would be the right time to accept Christ. The fact of the matter is we can never get ourselves ready. My list of sins was long, but the Bible says, *"we all have sinned and fall short of the glory of God"* (Romans 3:23, NIV). We are all equals!

135

God loves us and wants us to walk in our destiny here on earth and then live with Him forever in Heaven. So when He sent His only son, Jesus, to die on the cross *for our sins*, He was giving each of us the chance to be washed clean (forgiven forever!) and to walk in our destiny. It has all been done for us; all we need to do is take Him up on His offer.

Will you? You have a destiny that only God could have imagined for you! Everyone will eventually arrive at a destination in life, but a destination is a far cry from walking in your destiny! Once you have fulfilled your time on earth, where will you then spend eternity? Take the first step now and do as I did, accept Christ as your Lord and Savior. Enter into the goodness He has for you in ALL AREAS of your life. With a simple confession and believing in your heart, you can enter into His family, my family, and know for certain where you will spend eternity when this life is over. That's the legacy He left for you.

ACTION STEPS TO GET YOU THERE

ACCEPTING HIS OFFER

In the Word of God it says that if you confess with your mouth that Jesus is Lord and believe in your heart that God raised Him from the dead, you will be saved (Romans 10:9). So confess now, out loud, that Jesus is the Son of God and if you believe in your heart that God raised Him from the dead, you are now SAVED! If you have just completed those two steps, congratulations and welcome to the family!

Your life will never be the same from this moment on. I strongly recommend that you become affiliated with a local church and tell someone of your decision. They will be almost as excited as I am right now! Stay in the Word of God and submit to His Holy Spirit to lead, guide, and teach you in all things. Please write or e-mail us and tell us of your decision. It is the greatest gift we could receive.

Testimonies

"I came in contact with Henry a few years ago in a music shop. We went to school together about twenty years ago but we didn't keep in touch. He asked me how things were going and over the course of several meetings, I told him how my life had unraveled. I was on crank (a type of drug) and had been for the past six years. I lost my family, my relationships, my house, and my job. I was to the point where I was eating out of dumpsters. Henry met me one day at a hospital that I tried to check into instead of killing myself. I felt so hopeless and didn't know what to do. The staff at the hospital offered no help and told me to commit myself to a psych ward. Henry then prayed with me and I felt different immediately. We spent the next few days together and he taught me a new way of living. Over the next few weeks I was off crank, my family returned, I moved into a house, found a great job, and I was moving toward a career that before seemed impossible. 'Right' relationships were restored and I was eating food purchased from the grocery store. I don't know where I would be today if Henry had not been a part of my life. When I thank him, he gives God the glory. I would encourage anyone to listen to what this man has to say. It will change your life forever, just like it did mine."

—Marcello P.

"I met Henry at a local business and asked him, 'What does a guy have to do to drive a car like that?' He was driving his Mercedes®. Henry began telling me of the blessings of God upon his life and that God could do the same for me. He began teaching me balance and made sure I understood that life wasn't just about money. He said that if I aligned my life with the Word of God, then all the "things" that I desired would be added to me in balance. Within just a few weeks after talking with Henry and studying his teachings, my life totally changed. I wrote my vision down, just like he said and began taking the steps he told me about. I am proud to say that I have led the entire nation in sales for the past few months and my income has doubled. I am growing my own business now and just hired a man to be one of my regional vice-presidents. This same man hired me to work for the company he represented just a few months prior! My life is ACCELERATING! I always knew there was something great inside me, but the destination I was headed toward was not my destiny. I was living far beneath my potential. Henry showed me how to get the rubber on the road and begin fulfilling my divine destiny. I want to thank him so much for the wonderful work he is doing. Henry's teachings have literally taken my life from poverty to power!"

—Brent M.

AUTHOR CONTACT INFORMATION

If this book or workbook has been beneficial to you in any way, we would like to hear about it. You can write to us and/or send a tax deductible contribution to help continue this ministry at:

Henry A. Penix Ministries
P.O. Box 701320
Tulsa, OK 74170
Email: Henry@HAPM.com

For future information about the Henry A. Penix Ministries or to schedule a personal appearance at your church, business or conference, please contact us at:

Henry@HAPM.com
Fax (918)447-2772
www.HAPM.com

Do you know someone that could benefit from this book? If so, buy them a copy and send it now!

May God richly bless you in all that you do!